EMBERS AMONG THE ASHES

The Rise, Fall, and Rebirth of Religious Orders in the Church in America

Martin F. Larréy

TREATY OAK PUBLISHERS

PUBLISHER'S NOTE

This is a work of academic research based on the experiences of the author.

Printed and published in the United States of America

TREATY OAK PUBLISHERS

ISBN-978-1-943658-64-0

Available in print from Amazon

DEDICATION

In loving memory of my father, Martin Larréy, who passed away while working on this edition of the book. These pages reflect his love for the Church and her mission to evangelize all nations through personal sanctification.

It is my hope that the reader will come to share the same enthusiasm and desire that my father was blessed with to accept the moments of grace (as the Greeks would say, "Kairós") that God offers to everyone. May he rest in peace.

Fr. Philip Larréy

What is the vocation "crisis" in Catholic religious life and how can we understand it?

It has been customary for many years to lament the decline of religious vocations in the Catholic Church—both to the priesthood and to the consecrated life—and, depending on one's proclivity of view, either to lambaste the Church for its intransigence in thwarting the aspirations of women, homosexual men, and others from entering those forms of religious life to which they claim to be called, or to deplore what the writer perceives as the irretrievable decline of culture and civility and the scorching consequences of a secularism run rampant which simply shrivels the call for vocations. As is often the case, neither alleged explanation reckons with God's providential role in history.

While certainly on the level of *secondary causality*—in the workaday world in which we can see things happen for a reason and because of recognizable factors (the area in which the sciences shine) we are incapable of ever seeing God's direct intervention in the affairs of this world save in the case of verifiable miracles. These come, however, with such sufficient rarity that they are useless in an analysis of causality. We do need always to bear in mind that in terms of *primary causality*, God is calling forth creation [in all manner of ways about which we know nothing.[1] As a completely unfounded assertion…] Their idea of a vocation crisis is, "how can we handle all of these men and women?" One religious community in Michigan, the Sisters of Mary, Mother of the Eucharist, has made three additions to its motherhouse in recent years to accommodate vocations and is in the process of raising money to add another addition. The Poor Clare nuns of Irondale and Hanceville, Alabama, are constantly seeking new establishments to accommodate the continuous influx of young women to the religious life of the Poor Clare nuns.

The hand-wringing over vocations brings to mind the old joke about a drunk who lost his key while in the middle of an intersection and began looking for it around the lamppost on the sidewalk. An observer who saw all this came up to him and said, "What are you doing?" "I am looking for my key which I lost when I was crossing the street." "Well, why are you looking for it here," asked the observer. "Because the light is better over here," said the drunk. So it is with vocations; it depends on where you look for them.

Invariably, those who lament the failure of vocations focus on a couple of things; first, the decline of the numbers in the priesthood over the last twenty to thirty years; second, the precipitous decline of women in female religious communities.

There is also a dangerous and provincial myopia, which in focusing primarily on the Church in America, rashly infers that what has happened and is happening here is a reliable mirror of the church throughout the world. If one were to stand at the entrance of the Pontifical Lateran University in Rome for twenty minutes, one would clearly appreciate how *untypical* the Church in America is. Pouring from the gates of the Lateran is a snapshot of the Church Universal; men and women in about equal numbers and of every age and color—mostly black and brown, however—entering and leaving classes. Some are in clerical garb—flowing robed Dominicans and cassock-clad curates, nuns in full habits and just as many in sandals and slacks, and colorful dashikis and caftans add a riot of color; a panorama that is inconceivable at a typical American seminary.

There is no denying that a number of important factors negatively impacted religious life in America in the last two generations; these factors will be dealt with in a subsequent chapter. However, another important factor that will be dealt with later is how remarkably untypical the profile of religious life in the Church in America was at the midpoint of the last century.

For those who wish to make that the norm and compare the current rates of entrance to the religious life to those days, the comparisons will always fall short since the period of 1920–1960 of the Church in America in terms of the numbers in the priesthood and in religious life and the homogeneity of Catholic culture is probably the most idiosyncratic period in the two-thousand-year history of the Church, save for the third century in Egypt or the declining years of seventeenth-century Spain.

So, in addition to the question of absolute decline (which is incontrovertible), there is the notion of *relative* decline. Because the circumstances of the Church in America in the 1950s were unique to that particular period and all of those circumstances have passed away, it is unrealistic to use numbers from that period as a barometer of contraction or expansion. Certainly, compared to that period, the generations of the 1840s and

1850s or of the 1880s and 1890s experienced a serious "crisis" of vocations since the numbers of Catholics during those periods grew and exceeded in ratios the number of professed religious and priests by several orders of magnitude.[2]

Moreover, what casts a pall of gloom over the conversation about the vocation crisis is that everyone knows (and the actuarial tables are there for the dim-witted or those in denial) that the current decline among the historic and major religious communities in America will continue to decline until the number reaches zero. So in some sense the cries of "Wolf! Wolf!" regarding the decline of vocations is only part about the decline.

It is also an enduring lament that those great institutions that did so much to create the Church in America in the nineteenth and twentieth centuries—the Sisters of Charity, the Sisters of Notre Dame, the Sisters of Mercy, the Sisters of St. Joseph, the Society of Jesus, the Congregation of the Most Holy Redeemer, the Society of the Sacred Heart of Jesus, and dozens of variants of Dominicans and Franciscans—are all passing away, as ineluctably as the Beguines and the anchorites of the Syrian desert did so many centuries ago, never to return.

And since for the great community of Catholics in America of a certain age, the early associations with one or more of these congregations shaped an entire cultural outlook and even a way of life, their passing is poignant and deeply saddening.

So we must disenthrall ourselves of the natural but erroneous belief that the Church in which Catholics in America of recent generations grew mirrored the face of the Church around the world. It was, on the contrary, a special and historically structured culture in much the same way Byzantine

Christianity was from Justinian until the fall of Constantinople in 1453. But, as one cultural experience passes away a new one struggles to be born. The burden of this book will be to describe those new forms.

What follows is basically a book in two parts. In part one we will deal, in succession, with the rise of religious communities, principally of women, in the modern world from the time of the Counter-Reformation through the French Revolution. We will follow those communities in their efflorescence and decline in the nineteenth and twentieth centuries with specific reference to the Church in America. The last part of this first half will articulate the origins, development, and theology of personal reform from the time of St. Paul to St. Augustine, the various permutations it took, and how it achieved a synthetic whole.

The second part of the book will examine how out of the general dissolution of historic religious communities in the United States in the closing decades of the twentieth century and the creeping spread of social decay, new charisms are blooming and attracting young men and women to new apostolates following spiritual paths not unlike those taken by the earliest men and women of the Christian era who fled to the desert to live a life *with and for* Christ almost two thousand years ago in order to "renew the face of the earth" and sanctify all creation.

The rhythm of reform in the Church is another of those constants like the never-knowable number of vocations being proffered by God at any given time. Ever since Jesus declared "that we must be perfected, even as our heavenly father is perfect," there have been men and women who have abandoned the ways of the world and sought out means by which to strive toward that perfection in whatever and by whatever means lay at hand.

And as should be no surprise to anyone, often the means at hand vary dramatically from the practices of the existent communities. For example, the poor, sick, and destitute of Calcutta certainly clogged the streets of that city long before Mother Teresa began her work among them; one could hardly maintain she "discovered" them. But before her, no one ever saw them quite as clearly as Christs to be loved as she did.

There were certainly scads of religious communities in that part of the world—who in some cases had been there for centuries including the Sisters of Loreto, the community to which Mother Teresa belonged—who certainly were not unmindful of the need. What occurred was the gift of a new charism; a special grace illuminating a soul to start something new by which Christ could be made manifest to the world. This charism came through Christ's direct intervention in the life of St. Teresa of Calcutta, calling her to take care of him who was among the poor.

To take another venue, at the end of the last century the Church hierarchy knew it was essential to engage modern evangelization through the emerging electronic media. In fact, the need was so clear that the bishops mandated a national collection in support of communications and media outreach. Simultaneously, countless dioceses embraced brow-raising debt to launch television stations and radio programming. Yet it would be hard, using even the simplest of benchmarks, to ascertain any significant impact that all of this has had in recent years. The millions that have been spent have borne little fruit while creating yet another money-consuming bureaucracy in the Church. Yet when Mother Angelica trundled down to Alabama in 1962 with a few hundred dollars and started selling fish lures by mail to support her catechetical mailings, who would have prophesied what was to come? Later when she saw St. Michael on the hardscrabble peak of an isolated mountaintop where she set up a radio station contrary to all the principles of effective radio transmission, she launched a communication empire that now girds the globe, 24/7, in many languages, and has changed the lives of millions of people bringing them ever closer to Christ. This is an example of a new charism.[3]

Here is a third example. The nation has long been aware of—and embarrassed by—the rank desolation and emptiness of the South Bronx in New York City. The evidence of a large neighborhood in the stages of advanced physical decay, social disaggregation, and spiritual disorder has reverberated off the ears and eyes of Americans for more than a generation. Its gritty reality has been splayed across the movie screen, it has ferried countless sociological dissertations to successful defenses, and has larded the pages of the *New York Times* in recurring tut-tuts of civic failure and societal neglect. That this should transpire in what is arguably the premiere archdiocese of the Church in America, at least by status and history if not by right, teeming with hundreds of parishes, legions of priests and religious men and women, and yet still remain unattended should not be a surprise to anyone no less than the destitute of Calcutta were hardly invisible before Mother Teresa began gathering the wretched of the earth and helping them die. Yet nothing was done about it until the arrival of the

Community of the Franciscan Friars of the Renewal (CFR).

Yet it is clear that these men are not social workers, community organizers, or a political faction. They are men who are taking seriously once again the exhortation Christ gave to St. Francis to "Rebuild my house."

The San Damiano cross has been around since the early thirteenth century when St. Francis mistook Christ's command to literally rebuild the Church of San Damiano rather than to see his "house" as the Church itself. The San Damiano cross reflects off the walls of hundreds of Franciscan establishments around the world.

It has now reenergized a forlorn neighborhood by a singular focus to restore the presence of Christ in a place from which he had long been dispossessed and to do it in a way to deepen the spiritual affinity of a community of men to him. The priorities of the community are clear and can be grasped by noting the announcement posted to the doors of the friary: The poor seeking food and shelter are *not* to ring the bell for assistance when the monks are at prayer. It is a case of first things first.

Why are the CFRs growing in vocations? Why are young men flocking to be part of a community whose daily lives are surrounded with the walking wounded and spiritually deracinated of New York's lost souls? Why has the experience of these men enriched them to be spiritual counselors, retreat masters, and authors of books on the spiritual life?

Because as the founders of countless religious communities attest, that is where Christ is most visible to them, where the dramatically end-times scene of the closing chapters of St. Matthew's Gospel are most vividly portrayed and where the call to sanctity, and hence, service can be exercised daily and in an uncluttered way.

None of these groups nor dozens of others with whom we will become familiar in succeeding pages achieved "success" without struggle, and, most especially, without faith in what Christ was calling them to do, principally *to come to him, first*, and then to do it in a particular way, which, in fact, may be one with which the respondent may not even have the skills. No one with all the time in the world would have considered Mother Angelica to be tech savvy to the point of building, almost single-handedly, a billion-dollar enterprise while the whole institutional Church in America, on the other hand, struggled and labored—with expertise at its beck and call—to create a national communications systems seems to have very little evangelical impact.

The ineffable mystery of the relation of Christ to each of us lies beyond the reach of human methods of discovery, yet common sense compels us to be modest in our judgment when the tools of our inquiries are frail and terribly small. If a religious community insists on participating in adoration of the Eucharist daily for two hours by all of its members *before* they do a lick of work of any other kind, and their numbers mushroom while another religious community whose members are seldom found in a chapel, let alone at prayer, are declining, we certainly cannot infer any *causality* in terms with which that word is used in human inquiry. We can, however, observe that it is certainly a mighty interesting set of discrete facts that prompts a sense of curiosity.

The nostrums and platitudes of secularism have permeated our culture even to the point of shaping our outlook, mental habits, and affective drives. The shibboleths of the nineteenth century have triumphed everywhere: the workaday world in which we live is *the* pervasive reality; the mechanistic principles of natural science are advanced without question as the surest way of determining the facts of a matter; we have all become casual materialists; we are admonished to feel mild discomfort in discussing such things as "what is true"; it is contended that religious beliefs are, at best, plausible and personal aspirations, desires, fears, what have you, of each person regardless of their truth value; a genuine modernistic bias (as Pius X defined it) has settled into our very bones and we are disenthralled of it by only the most threatening of realities.[4]

Like the Athenians conversing with St. Paul in the Acts of the Apostles, we are amused, even jaded, and mildly curious about far-reaching claims about the nature and journey of human destiny. The dissonances in our souls are accepted as a matter of fact. We watch live the horrible slaughters perpetrated daily in Darfur or the Congo or elsewhere... and then go into supper and talk with conventional gravity about what we are going to wear tomorrow to work or school.

So that brings me to my next point: the cosmological scope of this work. At the current time, there is a kind of a renaissance going on in the field of apologetics, that branch of theology that deals with the defense of the Faith. A whole generation of young "reverts" and converts have broken into print, filled the airwaves, stood word-to-word on the debating floor, spun out DVDs, created packets and dozens of other things to "give witness to the faith that is in them," challenging all comers about the truth content of the Catholic Faith, and, directly or indirectly, assaulting those propositions I have just described about the style of the current age.

They are doing an admirable job, at least as demonstrated by the conversion tables, in calling to account the skeptic, the doubter, the truculent, the scientistic, the fundamentalist, the *sola scriptura* folks, the secularist, and dozens of other people who approach Catholic Christianity and the Church with arrogance, hesitancy, fear, anger, self-righteousness, or sheer human ignorance.

It is refreshing to see them do their work with knowledge, grace, and care. But I am going to ignore it all because the nature of this inquiry begins long after they have concluded their work.

We are simply going to begin on the assumption of the wholeness and intimate connection of this world and the next: the fundamental datum of theology that God is the source and sum of all reality and that he has a unique relationship with every human being that has been, is, or will ever exist because he has made each of us out of nothingness and sustains us at every moment of our lives from falling back into nothingness out of love alone.[5]

Further, that Jesus Christ is the Word—the only Word—of God and that in him, a real man and a Divine Person, and him alone is where one can find the source and summit of eternal life and that he continues to act at every moment in every human being's life from its beginning until its end. In a sense, while it may be useful in an instrumental way to posit a sharp distinction between immanence and transcendence—this world and the next—for our purposes we need to be mindful that that is a human construct to serve limited ends and contingent actions, but it is a faulty rendition of the nature of reality.

The ultimate unity of all reality is often found in the writings of the saints, many who maintained long and continuing conversations with Christ. For example, when one reads St. Teresa of Ávila's *Autobiography*, one is struck by the casualness and intimacy of her dialogues with Christ, in her many visions, carried on in the same language she used with the Sisters.

This work will further presume the rest of the major affirmations of the Christian religion: the inerrancy of scripture, the reality of the Resurrection of Jesus and his establishment of a Church to endure until the end of the world, the integrity of whose teaching is vouchsafed by divine authority itself. Also, we accept as fact that for his own purposes, Christ calls certain individuals from time to time to a life of heroic virtue to continue the work of universal redemption of all human beings and the sanctification of all creation.

Last but certainly as important, some observations on the nature of the *moral life* as that phrase is used in this work. At the outset, we can dismiss particular explanations of morality such as those of Richard Rorty, Peter Singer, and others in contemporary ethical studies who advocate a radical, individualist philosophy that insists that ethical principles are not something universally true and abiding, but, in fact, are *only* individualized *constructions* of reality designed to facilitate each person's own choices irrespective of any truth value they might have.[6]

This critical school of ethical thought effectively posits that a human being is an autonomous, exclusively rationalist monad which fabricates a uniquely personal ethical system to meet the needs, fears, and beliefs as each person conceives those, and that there are no creditable philosophical tools by which anyone can make comparative evaluations and judgments of competing ethical world views.

Mercifully, many people do not seriously consider using this approach in raising small children or governing a nation, in falling in love or building skyscrapers. The consequences would be catastrophic.

There is a kind of shunning-common-sense and a flight-from-reality aspect to this approach as well. In one of his conferences, Fr. Bryan Hehir pointed out that, in fact, each person's life is a tissue of dynamic *relationships*.[7] We come into the world without our own permission; we are sustained (or not) by family and then friends; we are connaturally aware that we have a past which we had no role in creating but which is nonetheless ours and a future whose shape will be made by people and circumstances over which, in many cases, we have little or no control.

We also know that these relationships entail *obligations*, not discretionary, autonomous, rational choices. Often in how well or poorly we acquit ourselves of these obligations will determine peace or disorder of not only our own lives but of numerous other people. We come into existence in a place and time with many ties and obligations, and therefore, with a *structure* of lines of action (the need for compassion and assistance for an invalid parent or sibling, for example).

We are equally aware that there is a concomitant *structure* of how to evaluate the alternatives of those choices in terms of value and consequence. For thousands of years, the study of the science of ethics consisted in a lengthy meditation on illuminating the nature and purpose of those structures. As will be noted below, Aristotle's *Nicomachean Ethics* is one of the first and finest expositions on the teleological nature of the moral life.

The irruption of Christianity dramatically distended the scope and finality of the moral life (as will be detailed later) by bypassing the perennial search for means to attain human integrity and human happiness. Christianity affirmed the end of each human being to be nothing less than as a son or daughter of God structured to be with him in eternal bliss.

This was best served up aphoristically by St. Augustine in his famous statement in *The Confessions*, "Our hearts are restless, God, until they rest in you."

Christianity thus inverted the focus of the ethical meditation from inward to outward, from a careful analysis of the relative merits of our choices to affect our own journey toward human happiness to probing into the means by which to find and then to pursue the journey of God. It is a journey, Christianity in unyielding fashion affirmed at the same time that was one we could not complete by our own efforts. Christianity thus held out a new, dazzling goal for the human journey … that was perpetually out of reach. In the broadest sense, the history of personal reform in Christian history is the story of men and women finding in an intimate relationship with Christ the means to attain that end. How this evolved over an extensive period of centuries will be taken up in chapters IV and V.

It may seem unnecessary to say all this, but it is merely to forestall natural but irrelevant questions. In the same sense that when one is mesmerized by the drama of a squeeze bunt play in the eighth inning of a tied ballgame with two on in the seventh game of a World Series, to ask the question, "How do we know what we are seeing is real?" is an irrelevant question.

In sum, there are doubts about the so-called vocation

crisis described in the opening paragraphs of this chapter. We will review the evolution of the theology of personal reform and the specific ways it manifested itself first in the religious communities of the Counter-Reformation of the sixteenth and seventeenth centuries and then in the Catholic Revival of the nineteenth century. We will examine the peculiar nature of Catholic culture in America over the last hundred and fifty years and the men and women who shaped it to make it what it was and is and led to the crisis in which we find ourselves.

In the conclusion of the first half, we will examine the foundations and long maturation process of the idea of personal reform in Christian theology, starting with selected passages in the Pauline Epistles and evolving through the meditations of the early fathers, culminating in the works of St. Augustine.

The second part of the book will canvas the revival of new religions communities in light of that perennial understanding of personal reform and how its revival shunts aside the architecture of religious motivation and reform as these were practiced in the nineteenth and twentieth centuries.

Let us now turn to the origin, development, and decline of Catholic religious orders in the modern age.

II

The Rise and Fall of Religious Communities since the Renaissance

In order to understand the impetus for new religious communities emerging around us, it is necessary to understand the decline of the traditional religious communities that have been prominent over the last centuries. But to focus on that question, it is further necessary to tell two distinct stories about the evolution of religious communities in the modern world.

First, it is essential to contrast those religious communities established before the French Revolution with those established in the nineteenth century *after* the Revolution. It is hard to exaggerate the decisive impact of the Revolution on all aspects of Catholic Christianity. The manner in which it affected the character and outlook of those religious communities established in post–1815 Europe, especially France, is of vital importance to understand the prominent religious orders that first waxed in the immigrant Church in America and which are now in precipitate decline. For the vast majority of them, with few exceptions, originated in the early nineteenth century in the midst of or in the wake of the passing of the Revolution and the Napoleonic Wars that followed.

The distinct but related factor that needs to be examined

is the particular sociohistorical context in America of the immigrant nineteenth and early twentieth-century Church from which these orders were to draw thousands of members in the period from 1880 to around 1960. In other words, there were certain social, familial, and national characteristics of that unique span of time that both propelled men and women into religious life and the priesthood which, however, failed to ground them trenchantly in the foundational suppositions of a genuine spiritual life.

When the turmoil of the 1960s and 1970s afflicted these priests, brothers, and sisters, the searing challenges laid bare the weaknesses of their founding religious communities as well as the weaknesses of their own specific formation. We will discuss this series of dramatic events in chapter III.

The Religious Orders of the Catholic Reformation

It is well to remember, as Hans Hillerbrand reminded us, that whatever else of drastic note the Reformation and the Counter-Reformation were about—new modes of thought, the emergence of the nation-state, economic convulsions, and the development of commercial and proto-industrial organizations—they were first and foremost about fundamental religious issues.[8] What is the anatomy of personal reform?

What is the correct view of soteriology, that is, our understanding of salvation? What is the deposit of faith? How is it determined and accessed? How is its meaning ascertained? What is the nature of the sacraments? What is the new asceticism? What is the relationship, if any, between human actions and the economy of salvation?

The titanic struggles of the sixteenth and seventeenth centuries by pen, oratory, printing presses, and finally, guns and armies were efforts to answer those questions and then either to restore them to the religious life of the European Continent or to establish a new dispensation of the Christian religion.

From the polemics and disputations of Melanchthon and Eck in the 1520s to the final signings of the treaties of Westphalia in 1648, Europeans on almost all levels spent over a century drafting and redrafting answers to these questions and attempting to preserve the integrity of Christian theology and ensure its triumph across the face of Europe.

In the end, neither side achieved its purpose.

Since my purpose is to concentrate on Catholic religious communities, we will leave the further development of Protestantism to another book and turn our attention to the dramatic events within the Catholic or Counter-Reformation Church that became the nursery of some of the greatest religious communities since the founding of Monte Cassino in 529.

We often need reminding that the rise of Protestantism was not a sudden flash of light in a mute and murky world. The fifteenth century was awash with religious mystics, cranks, group revivalists, and bizarre sects. So it is natural that the sixteenth and seventeenth centuries were suffused with religion.

On the one hand was a continent-wide clash of conflicting understandings of the principal elements of the Christian religion, and on the other, a series of distinctly creative trends in search of personal sanctification, some of which antedated the rise of Luther. These would often overlap or mutually impact each other, but for long-term purposes, the latter was the more positive and enduring consequence of the religious ferment. It is well to remember that religious stirrings such as the founding of the Theatines and the formative experiences of St. Ignatius and the first Jesuits in Paris had nothing to do with the rise of Protestantism.

In fact, St. Ignatius, like St. Francis before him, was strongly committed to a pilgrimage to the Holy Land and was almost entirely consumed with efforts to emulate the life of Christ in a new and profound way. We must remember as well that it was purely by accident that the Society of Jesus came to be the exemplars of modern classical Catholic education.

The establishment of the Roman College by St. Ignatius was principally for the education and formation of novices of the Society. Only when its remarkably integrated and sophisticated blend of advanced classical studies and Christian theology proved to be such a potent weapon in, first, creating an articulate Catholic apologetic and then, demonstrating the social value of classical letters in a modern context that the Society acceded to the wishes of the Holy See to permit non-Jesuits to enroll.

Two other examples will suffice to demonstrate that the stirrings of religious reform were a common element at the turn of the sixteenth century even before the age of religious controversy. In the closing decades of the fifteenth century, St. Catherine of Genoa, a laywoman who never joined a religious community, became an exemplar in caring for the sick in Genoa and through a life of fierce prayer and daily communion (something unheard of at the time) brought about remarkable changes in health care in Genoa as well as effected the conversion of her profligate, sadistic husband into a third order Franciscan.

In 1525, Matteo da Bascio, a conventual Franciscan, was appalled that so many of his brethren were not living the rule of St. Francis. His efforts to live a life of strict poverty and to care for the poor were strenuously resisted by ecclesiastical authorities but, eventually, Clement VII granted his group the right to have their own rule and to live in hermitages. They came to be known as the Capuchins. Again, this is but another example of the strong desire of countless people craving for and seeking out a more intimate life with Christ with little or no consideration of the larger public world in which they found themselves. It is from this perspective that one can plausibly argue that the Counter-Reformation actually began before the Reformation itself.

For all the variety of the religious orders that began in the Counter-Reformation, they shared a common focus on spiritual renewal and personal sanctification. The Theatines, the Jesuits, the Ursulines, the Vincentians, the Capuchins, the reformed Carmelites, the Redemptorists, and the Trappists were principally committed to reknitting, in a new setting, the ties between the individual and Christ.

"I will follow like a puppy dog if I can only find a way to salvation" is how St. Ignatius of Loyola put it. This could serve as the banner words of all the reformers from the 1500s to the death of St. Alphonsus Liguori in 1787.

Whether one considers the mystical theology of St. Teresa of Ávila, the missionary zeal of St. Francis Xavier, the *Introduction to the Devout Life by St. Francis de Sales, the Spiritual Exercises* of St.

Ignatius, the innovations concerning priestly formation by the Oratory at St. Sulpice, the devotions to the Sacred Heart by St. Margaret Mary Alacoque, or the teaching of poor girls by St. Angela Merici and the Ursulines—the overarching purpose was fundamentally the same: to articulate a means by which one could establish and nurture an intimate relationship with Christ.

We often miss this essential fact when we view these events principally in an instrumental way. For example, St. Angela is repeatedly lauded for several innovations. She drew laywomen together without the benefit of cloister; she taught young girls, which was unheard of, and did it for free; the members of her community lived in their respective homes and not in community, and so on.

What are seldom mentioned are the ecstatic visions in which Christ called her to himself; as she repeatedly stressed to her companions, it was not the work that she and they performed that was important, but it was the sustained Christocentric prayer life that *made* it important.

Likewise, we hallow the work of the Jesuits in founding a network of impressive *colegios* throughout Europe and eventually around the world. They were feared and respected as the great defenders of the traditional Church and the papacy as well as for their dramatic scientific work and missionary explorations. They were the counselors of kings and the confessors of queens.

As mentioned above, none of this was important to St. Ignatius and the first Jesuits. What was important could be found in the *Spiritual Exercises*; its heart is the choice of the two banners: Christ or Satan, which forms the core of the second week of the Exercises. Everything *before* the choice is in preparation for making the choice and everything *after* concerns the consequences of having made the choice.

The Exercises were intended to be transformational. The watchwords of the Society of Jesus, after all, are *Ad maioram Dei gloriam*—for the greater glory of God—which sanctifies the work not for its own value but because it reflects the glory of God.

As we shall see in a subsequent chapter, the lineaments of this relationship of the individual to God had been tested by fiery trials and controversies in the first three centuries of the Catholic Church's history. It was not until the time of St. Augustine that a mature and sophisticated concept of personal renewal was established.

But in the dissolution of the Middle Ages and the excesses of the Renaissance Church, the spirit of renewal either withered away or took eccentric and often erratic forms. The last half of the fifteenth century, much like the last third of the twentieth century, was marked by sectarian, ersatz, and bizarre religious behaviors and activities, fortunately with little staying power.

What the Counter-Reformation religious communities attempted—and did so with considerable success—was to exemplify in their own lives, and through a whole series of instruments, how to live a supernatural life in relation to the Trinity but most especially with Jesus Christ, the God-man.

Whether it was through an annual thirty-day retreat with the *Spiritual Exercises*, the nine First Fridays devotion of St. Margaret Mary, the radical austerity of the monks at La Trappe, the goal was always to insist on one of the fundamental goals of Counter-Reformation spirituality; that is, a personal relationship with Christ, the efficacy of prayer, discipline and mortification, the eager embrace of an incarnational Christology with a palpable in-the-flesh Jesus at its center, the mysterious but comfortably affirmed belief that each of us has a vital role to play in our own sanctification and, indeed, of the whole world.

Again, St. Ignatius summed it up in his pithy aphorism: "Work as if everything depended on you, and pray as if everything depended on God."

To appreciate the significant impact of all these movements on the face of European culture, one needs only to contrast the features of architecture, urban life, education, types of devotions, and so forth between the Medieval and Baroque. The differences can often be traced to the impact of a specific religious community. For example, we associate a particular style of monastic architecture with the rise of the Cistercians in the twelfth century. No less decisively did the Jesuits raise dozens of baroque churches on four continents.

Different communities sought the goal of personal renewal through different apostolates; for example, teaching, caring for the sick and orphaned, energizing parish life, forming men into holy priests, ranging across the lands giving missions, or holing up in some deserted and drafty monastery to labor and pray in perpetual silence. This is not to discount the profound impact these communities had on the general European population (not to overlook as well the cultures of South and Central America, India and the Far East).

Ironically, for all their focus on individual renewal, it was the Counter-Reformation orders that truly made Catholic Christianity a worldwide institution. The Counter-Reformation validated the ancient spiritual truism: *if you first change yourself, you can change the world.*

While the generation of giants of the Counter-Reformation came to an end with the death of Armand de Rancé (1700), founder of the Trappist Cistercians, St. Louis de Montfort (1716), priest and missionary apostolic, and St. Alphonsus Liguori (1787), founder of the Redemptorists, the spirit of the Counter-Reform perdured to the time of the French Revolution.

In fact, contrary to an often-asserted claim that the eighteenth century was the age of reason, par excellence, writers such as Derek Beales maintain that the eighteenth century should more accurately be described as the "Christian century."[9] Though there were some conspicuous cases of worldly prelates, and some historians like to point out that on the eve of the Revolution all of the members of the hierarchy of France were from the nobility—a datum of sociology, not religiosity, I would suggest—the Church was by and large in a healthy state, even in France.

Certainly eighteenth-century Catholicism in its architecture, especially in the German Empire and the Hapsburg lands, in its recurring pilgrimages, and the widespread vitality of religious confraternities and devotionals evince the enduring and benignant impact of the Counter-Reformation secular clergy and religious orders. Probably at no time since the apogee of Byzantine Christianity had the Church achieved such a pervasive and wholesome impact on the culture of which it was the informing and constitutive spirit.

Throughout Catholic Europe up until the upheavals of the French Revolution and the Napoleonic Wars, the cycles of life, the feast days and fast days, the seasons of the year, and the daily activities of the vast majority of men and women were shaped and sustained by the architectonic structure of the Catholic view of the world and the next.

Setting aside the political, economic, and social factors that precipitated the onset of the Revolution—and however worthy or unworthy these factors were in precipitating it—the fact remains that for Catholic Christianity and the millions who were shaped by its teachings, rituals, strictures, festivals, and aspirations, the Revolution was to prove an unmitigated disaster.

In the welter of passions unleashed by the economic crisis France faced in the winter and spring of 1789, a small stream of virulent anticlericalism, nurtured principally by the *philosophes* through the last half of the eighteenth century, morphed under the explosive stresses of 1789–1791 into full-blown anti-Christianity with principal focus on the Catholic community, its leadership, and institutional apparatus.

These views were seldom found among the vast number of peasants in the towns and villages of the countryside but were deeply imbibed in by those members of the bourgeoisie who were attorneys, journalists, small merchants, and elements of the justice system along with some disenchanted members of the clergy who, frankly, used their positions for personal advancement and whose religiosity was, for all purposes, long gone; precisely the nonaristocratic social elites who were to play a disproportionately large role in the grim days of the early 1790s.

The opening salvo between the new rationalist and secularist ideology and Catholic Christianity was the Civil Constitution of the Clergy, passed in July 1790 by the National Assembly of

France, which had evolved in the summer of 1789 out of the initial sitting of the Estates General. The Civil Constitution was an emulsion of different and often incompatible elements: part genuine organizational reforms, part naiveté, mixed with dollops of cynicism and greed with a spoonful of indifference. Tellingly, the principal author of the Civil Constitution was Charles Maurice de Talleyrand-Périgord, the onetime bishop of Autun, a man of no discernible religious beliefs.

To the well-meaning, it was an attempt to fuse the Church into the revolutionary concept of the nation; in effect, to "nationalize" the Church, to achieve in some sense the long-thwarted aspiration of the Gallican Church. With grudging acceptance, the bishops in France acceded to the expropriation of Church lands, the sale of which was to serve as collateral for defraying the national debt.

However, there were other features of the Civil Constitution that were unacceptable: the abolishment of all the ancient dioceses of the kingdom and reconfiguring each diocese to coincide with the newly designed administrative departments; the election of bishops by departmental constituents and without authorization from Rome; the dissolution of the monastic orders; and finally, the imposition of an oath on all the clergy demanding their allegiance to the nation and, after September 1793, the Republic.

These latter features created a crisis of conscience for many; not the least of whom was the king. Efforts were made to secure papal approval for the Civil Constitution and while he was at first hesitant to provoke a crisis, when the National Assembly passed it without Roman approval, Pius VI condemned it as an unacceptable intrusion into the internal governing structures of the Church in France.

The Civil Constitution became the immovable wedge that drove the Revolution, internally, to cycles of increased radicalism vis-à-vis the Church. For the small but vocal Gallican Church party in France, with its long history of chafing under what it perceived to be alien Roman rule, it was the apotheosis so long eluded. For the ever-militant Jacobins—self-defined bearers of the new secular order—it was evident proof of the ill will and treachery of those who would undermine the chastening reforms of the Revolution.

To the many practicing Catholics and an overwhelming number of the bishops of France, it became the rallying cry against the excesses of the Revolution.

As the Revolution moved into more radical stages with the election of the National Convention in 1792 and the Jacobins (or "Mountain" as they were called because they sat on the highest seats on the left side of the Assembly) assumed virtual dictatorial power, the militant party was determined to extirpate the nonjuring clergy, that is, those who refused to take the oath of allegiance as prescribed in the Civil Constitution as well as to create a "republic of reason" on the ash heaps of Catholic Christianity.

Hundreds of clergy were summarily arrested. The Paris mob, which had been the principal instrument of intimidation used by the Jacobins at various critical points in the last eighteen months, was unleashed.

With the cry *La Patrie en danger* echoing through the ancient medieval streets of the city, the mob ransacked the prisons in the September Massacres and summarily murdered hundreds of clergy, including the Archbishop of Paris, along with numerous women and children who had been detained on suspicion of anti-revolutionary activities.

When the Revolution moved to its most extreme stage—the Reign of Terror (September 1793 with the Law of Suspects until July 28, 1794, the Thermidorian Reaction)—the government of the convention, virtually controlled by the Committee of Public Safety which was the instrument of Jacobin power, set out systematically to dechristianize the country and, most energetically, crush the uprising of the militant Catholics in the western region of La Vendée.[10]

One of the more graphically brutal events in the history of the Catholic Church in France was the assigning of Jean Baptiste Carrier as a representative on mission to La Vendée to suppress the insurrection. He executed thousands, many priests and religious, by loading them on floating barges in the Loire estuary and having them sunk. Several other thousands were simply taken out into the fields of the countryside and summarily shot, one by one, anticipating the butchery of many subsequent revolutionary movements down to the Khmer Rouge.

He was described as "one of those inferior and violent spirits, who in the excitement of civil wars become monsters of cruelty and extravagance." His brutality and indiscriminate slaughter failed to staunch the insurrection. As his excesses became known, he was recalled to Paris and, after the end of the Terror, was quickly tried, unanimously found guilty and guillotined.

I have spent time describing the salient features of the French Revolution as they impacted on the institutional Church and the millions of its members in France because it would be hard to exaggerate the devastation—economically, politically, spiritually, and psychologically on that Church and those people. In less than a handful of years, an ancient Catholic community whose public religious life encompassed a vast complex of monasteries, abbeys, schools, orphanages, health facilities, famous shrines and dioceses and whose existence stretched back in time to when the Roman Legions still encamped on the banks of the Seine—all had been smashed, desecrated, and eradicated.

Churches had been turned into stables and warehouses, monasteries of great antiquity housing manuscripts of incalculable value had been looted and burned, communities of religious men and women had been sent wholesale to the guillotine, and thousands of parishes lay forlorn and unstaffed or presided over by priests who had taken the oath to the constitution and who had been foisted off on parishioners who accepted them with sullen inattention and poorly disguised contempt.

Two examples suffice.

The complex of buildings known as the Abbey of Cluny in Burgundy, founded in 910 and one of the great centers of Benedictine reform in the Middle Ages, was plundered in 1790 and sold off by the government. A good part of the structures served as a ready-made quarry for construction in the nearby town. What remains today, impressive as it is as ruins, represents only about ten percent of the original foundation.

Similarly, the great Abbey of Citeaux founded in 1098 and the flagship of another great example of the Benedictine reform, which spawned a network of Cistercian monasteries across all of Europe, was depopulated and sold. The deteriorating structure passed through several hands, experiencing advancing stages of decay, until at the close of the nineteenth century the Trappists were able to buy it and begin the process of restoration.

The dislocation caused by the French Revolution was by no means limited to France. The disappearance of the entire Holy Roman Empire in 1806, apart from how desiccated its political apparatus had become, eradicated the ecclesiastical and public life of the Church in much of Germany no less there than it had in France.

The same cycle of expropriations, lootings, and destruction followed in the wake of the triumphant French armies wherever they went, carrying the new secular religion of the secular state. Equally catastrophic was the conquest and wholesale looting of the Italian Peninsula, including the capture of Rome and the abduction of the pope. It is said that the trail of wagons of the Napoleonic armies carrying the spoliation of a thousand churches, libraries, and art galleries stretched for miles wending its way over the Alps back to France. Pius VI was forcibly taken from Rome to Siena then to Florence, and then over the Alps to Valence where he died (1799) at the age of eighty-two.

More than one pundit hastened to announce smugly that the papacy had finally come to an end. However, it did not end.

His successor, Pius VII, elected in a conclave held in Venice under the protection of the House of Hapsburg, fared little better. Compelled to witness the coronation of Napoleon as emperor, Pius VII was later seized in 1809 by French troops and forcibly brought back to Fontainebleau and then to Savona, Italy, and was liberated to return to Rome only on the occasion of Napoleon's fall in 1814.

In spite of the Concordat of 1801 between Napoleon and

Pius VII, the recovery and restoration of the Church in France would take a lifetime or more. In many of the rural areas, *la France profonde*, religious life virtually stopped after 1793. When John Vianney was appointed the *Curé d'Ars* in 1818, he learned that d'Ars had not had a priest for over twenty years. For all intents and purposes, the community had reverted to paganism.

The period of the Restoration in France (1815–1830) was bedeviled by the intractable conflicts between the legatees of the Old Regime, once more in power, and the disgruntled heirs of the Revolution, each trying to find a way to sustain the values each side held dear.

Complicating matters was the nascent industrial and commercial revolutions that were beginning in France built around the development of textiles, mining, banking, and the manufacture of industrial and agricultural tools. The world that Dickens described for England in the first half of the nineteenth century was no less true for parts of Northern and Eastern France.

The social stresses of this new social order, being birthed in pain and with tragedies, was also dramatized in such works as *Les Miserables* by Victor Hugo.

Even before the conclusion of the Napoleonic Wars, efforts emerged to reconstitute an effective response to the havoc of revolution and war. In the midst of the trials of the end of the eighteenth century, a rebirth was taking shape that would swell to a flood tide of renewal. It reached such a magnitude that it can rightly be called the Catholic Revival of the nineteenth century.

It would be marked by the emergence of a spate of new religious orders—many of them French—and a resumption of the great missionary activities of the Church which had ended, for all practical purposes, by the end of the seventeenth century.

The Post-Revolutionary Foundations

There were a couple of features of this revival that deserve closer scrutiny since they were to be significant ingredients in the dissolution of the religious orders in the twentieth century and as well contribute—in some small part—to the dechristianization of Western culture.

One of the fatal legacies of the revolutionary upheaval, which was most dramatically embodied in the Concordat of 1801, was the belief that religion was essential to the stability of the state and its political life. It is a view that Napoleon emphatically espoused and implicitly one in which the hapless Pius VII had to acquiesce. Now, there is a clear demarcation between the notion that a religion was necessary and that a religion was true. As far as can be determined, Napoleon had no religious beliefs at all while enshrining religious institutions in the fabric of the social order.

He belonged to a growing number of that *intelligentsia* of the nineteenth century who reconceptualized religion as a bulwark of social order and stability against the anarchy and violence of revolution and messianic-like socialist theories that emerged in the 1820s and 1830s at the birth of the age of ideology—all the *isms* that continued to plague Western culture for the next century.

What followed, in effect, was the subservience of the public life of the Church to the dictates of the state. Even under the sympathetic times of the Restoration during the so-called union of throne and altar, it was a not always harmonious relationship. It was also to be a fateful one for the Church in France in the second half of the nineteenth century and the earliest decade of the twentieth.

The theory of religion as a kind of sociological glue essential to public order became widespread throughout nineteenth-century Europe, accelerated by the particular political theology of classical Protestantism and best epitomized by the Lutheran Churches in Scandinavia, the Anglican Settlement in England, or the Orthodox accommodation in Russia under Peter the Great and his successors.

In spite of heroic efforts by Pius IX and Leo XIII in subsequent years to extricate the Church from this relationship by articulating a modern version of the *libertas ecclesium* (freedom from secular power) that was prominent in the investiture struggle of the eleventh century, the other philosophy of state-Church relation endured and moved from triumph to triumph.

However worthwhile one may consider Pius VII's efforts to salvage the remnants of the Church in France from the depredations of war, savagery, and revolution while working from a position of little or no leverage, it may be argued that it condemned the Church to a subservient role in public life.

Thus, when it found itself at the end of the nineteenth century embroiled in controversy with the secularizing policies of the French Third Republic in the "revolt of the mayors," it became vulnerable to the final spoliation. When Pius X condemned the Law of Associations—which effectively laicized France through the closure of nearly eighty-five percent of all religious orders—and refused to submit the Church to the statutes governing "religious cults," all of the physical properties of the Church—its great cathedrals, monasteries, schools, hospitals, and the panoply of social institutions that had grown through the middle of the century—were expropriated and all subsidies in support of the Church ceased.

Relations between the Church and the state ended up almost as parlous at the end of the nineteenth century as they had been at the end of the eighteenth century.

The social glue theory of religion became a fundamental axiom of modern secular thought, touchingly rendered in America by the belief that people should be members of some organized religious body, the truth-value of its foundational propositions of little value, notwithstanding. In a metahistorical way, the history of the Catholic Church from the Syllabus of Errors to the Second Council can be perceived as a sustaining effort by the Church to once again assert its freedom from the political order.

The proclamation of the dogma of Papal Infallibility in 1870, coupled with the magisterial encyclical *Immortale Dei* by Leo XIII in 1885 on the relation of state to Church as the relationship of two "perfect" societies, were dramatic efforts to extricate the Church from its uncomfortable (and unfamiliar) role of being the moral suasion and social sedative of public life in a growing culture of absolutist nation-states.

It was not until the Second Council that the Church articulated a clear and mature vision of its independence vis-à-vis the world. Of course, the cataclysmic events of the twentieth century played no small role in effectuating and accelerating this change; in part, by liquidating the thousand-year-old lineaments of socioreligious culture that had sustained

Old Europe back to the age of the Carolingians, and, in part, by the denunciations of Nietzsche and Marx that the religion and religiosity of (principally Protestant and bourgeois) nineteenth-century Europe were hollow, meretricious, and fundamentally, sheer collusive social hypocrisy.

However, even at the nadir of Church fortunes in France in the closing years of the eighteenth century, the currents of renewal were stirring. Starting with the Society of the Sacred Heart of Jesus, founded by St. Madeleine-Sophie Barat in 1800 and the Sisters of Notre Dame de Namur by St. Julie Billiart in 1804 in Amiens, the first decades of the nineteenth century witnessed the emergence of dozens of new religious communities.

The Missionary Oblates of Mary Immaculate (1816), the Society of Mary (Marist Fathers) (1816), the Society of Mary (Marianist Brothers and Priests) (1817), the Congregation of the Holy Cross (1820), the Sisters of Mercy (1831), the Marists (Missionaries) (1832), the Daughters of the Cross (1833), the Sisters of Notre Dame (1843), the Society of the Catholic Apostolate or Pallottines (1845), the Institute of the Religious of the Sacred Heart of Mary (1849) are only the most prominent of the legion of religious communities that emerged in the first half of the nineteenth century.

Crowning, in a sense, this explosion of new foundations was the Society of St. Francis de Sales or the Salesians founded in 1855 by St. John Bosco. The Salesians grew rapidly throughout the world and became the third largest missionary community in the Church.

Moreover, many of these religious communities were to reach their efflorescence in the creation of the vast networks of institutions associated with bringing the Faith to the United States.

In contrast to the foundations associated with the Counter-Reformation Church, these new orders began and were shaped by an entire range of environmental and theological realities. Most strikingly and, in the long run, most decisively they came into existence to confront a baleful social landscape: wrecked social institutions for the poor and sick, scandalously few centers of education, especially for the young, and thousands of parishes without clergy or staffs. As Patricia Wittberg points out, the great motivation of the nineteenth-century communities was to address crying societal needs not to find or defend the correct path to personal sanctification as occurred in the sixteenth and seventeenth centuries.[11]

The dynamic of action was *outward* and not *inward*. If the architectonic holy grail of the Counter-Reformation was fundamentally a Christology that strove to open new channels of personal reform and sanctification; that aspired to be transformational in the arts, society, and indeed, the entire world, that of the Catholic Revival of the nineteenth century was to mitigate the tragedies that followed in the wake of revolution, war, and industrial exploitation and left a world scarred by profound social and political upheavals.

These new communities set out to instruct the ignorant, care for the sick, protect the orphan, and attend to the flotsam and jetsam that cluttered the social horizon as far as the eye could see. Probably no religious community—male or female—of the Catholic Revival typified this mission or succeeded as dramatically at it as the Sisters of Mercy. In one long generation they grew from a handful of Irish women to become one of the largest communities of religious women in the world, established in every continent around the globe within two brief generations.

They gave substance and power to modern medical practice by the creation of vast networks of hospitals; they were ubiquitous in dioceses around the world in staffing thousands of elementary and secondary schools, capping these accomplishments in the United States with over twenty colleges and universities. The parabola of their meteoric rise and then precipitous decline in the twentieth century may well serve as the signature piece of the great religious orders of the nineteenth century.

Their efforts were repeated time and again by the Sisters of St. Joseph, the Sisters of Notre Dame, the Franciscans and Dominicans. The upwelling of piety and the revival of religion that manifested itself in the midyears of the nineteenth century were very prolific in raising generations of young women and men who sensed a call to careers in making the corporal works of mercy available to larger and larger numbers of the uneducated, the poor, the sick, the marginalized, the orphaned.

What was to impel these new congregations onto the world's stage was not their growth or even their success in addressing the myriad social issues of nineteenth-century urban and industrial culture in Europe but a remarkable confluence of historical currents that was to provide a once-in-a-millennium opportunity. The waxing of the Catholic Revival coincided with the greatest migration of people in the history of the world as well as the apogee of the influence of Western civilization and the European states.

From the 1840s until the early decades of the twentieth

century, over sixty-five million people left Europe to find a better life ... somewhere; simultaneously, vast swathes of land came under the domination of Europe. The majority of these émigrés were Roman Catholics and the majority of them came to the United States. The elements were so poised as to create a remarkable and unique reality: a vast subculture of enormous proportions and profound historical consequences. A niagara of immigrants, a sparsely settled continent, a mildly hostile but tolerant populace, a neutral and non-interfering government, and an implacable determination to find a better life fused in creating the Catholic Church in America in the second half of the nineteenth century.

Because their social environment did not entail a titanic struggle over issues of soteriology, Christology, or eschatology, issues that formed the centerpieces of the Reformation and the Counter-Reformation, the theology of spiritual renewal and personal sanctification in the nineteenth-century revival was modest and almost all derivative. While the structures and models of organizations were different in the nineteenth century from the seventeenth century—after all, ninety percent of these new religious communities engaged in teaching of one kind or another or health care, professions difficult to wed to a cloistered existence—the underlying formation theology offered little that was new over the creative formularies of the seventeenth century.

Little was done to modify or update the process of spiritual formation in the novitiate or the seminary from what had been practiced in the seventeenth and eighteenth centuries. No creative nor innovative approaches to the spiritual life were gleaned from the changing circumstances of the social order.

Primacy centered on efforts to create a sense of community as some form of common life and to acquire the skill sets necessary to succeed in the social apostolate in which they were involved.

But, in great part, they followed formation practices of centuries ago and read the old masters of the spiritual life who struggled against different principalities and powers.

III

The Rise of the Church in the United States

The establishment and history of the Catholic Church in North America is, in a sense, a bifurcated story. In a way it was here with the first Europeans, and yet, in another way, it did not really arrive until the nation was on the cusp of becoming an industrial powerhouse in the latter half of the nineteenth century.[12]

Because of the ascendancy of France and Spain—the preeminent Catholic powers in Europe—in the period from 1500 to 1750, Catholic missionaries reached the periphery of what was to become the United States in the wake of French and Spanish settlements. Spanish friars roamed through the area from Florida to Virginia in the 1570s based on the Spanish settlement in St. Augustine, Florida. They were found in the earliest days of the settlement of Quebec at the turn of the seventeenth century, and they were in the vanguard of the Spanish establishment of Santa Fe, New Mexico, in 1598. New Orleans, founded in 1718, St. Louis in 1763, and San Francisco, established in 1776, all bore testimony to the presence of the Church on this continent.

Even before the founding of the Republic, Franciscans inched their way along the coast of California and established a string of missions from San Diego to Sonoma (1769–1823). It was the steady migration of the English to the Atlantic colonies and the worldwide triumph of British arms in the great wars of the mid-eighteenth century that ensured that the area that was to become the United States was to be overwhelmingly Protestant. The only toehold for Catholics in the early years of the development of America was the colony of Maryland; yet even here, within a century, the Catholics found they were a minority under a Protestant, tobacco-farming gentry.

Aside from Maryland, Catholics were also found in settlements in Pennsylvania, a great part due to the Quaker policy of religious tolerance. Yet, by and large, a deep and strong theme of anti-Catholicism coursed through the English colonies of the prerevolutionary era. From the steely Congregationalism of New England to the aristocratic Anglicanism of the Southern Colonies, everyone had an abiding revulsion for Roman Catholicism.

In most cases these colonies had explicit "state" churches and sedulously guarded the immigration of those beyond the pale such as Jews and Catholics. Among all of the benefits of the Revolution and American Independence, one of the most enduring to the Catholics was the formal establishment of religious freedom, eventually to be enshrined in the First Amendment to the US Constitution.

So, by the end of the eighteenth century and the beginning of the nineteenth, a Catholic presence became more evident. Often religious communities manifested this presence and, more striking, by women who were born in America. The Carmelites in Maryland, the Visitation nuns in Washington, DC, the Sisters of Loreto in Kentucky were the first examples.

The most famous, however, was the establishment of the Sisters of Charity in Emmitsburg, Maryland by St. Elizabeth Ann Seton in 1809. As Dolan points out, from the very beginning women in religious communities expressed a strong disinclination to shape their community life along the lines of the traditional modes found in Europe.

The fluid nature of early American public and cultural life, the lack of a strong tradition of enclosure for religious women, and the undeveloped nature of the structure of the hierarchical Church in America combined to create an ongoing tension between these early religious communities and the ecclesiastical authorities, often educated in France, who insisted on a more traditional mode of organization.[13]

The pre-immigrant Church in the United States was small, marginalized, and overwhelmingly European. There were no dioceses, schools, hospitals, social organizations, parishes, or seminaries. In 1800, Catholics constituted only one percent of the population of the new Republic. It was not until 1808 that an ecclesiastical province was created as the

Archdiocese of Baltimore with suffragan bishops in Philadelphia, New York, Boston, and Bardstown, Kentucky. This development owed a great deal to John Carroll who energetically resisted musings in Rome to appoint an apostolic delegate under the auspices of the Congregation for the Propagation of the Faith (the Propaganda).

With behind-the-scenes maneuvering of Benjamin Franklin, John Carroll himself was made the first bishop in the United States. Until that time much of the dispersed Catholic population had to sustain its own faith through communal gatherings, scripture study, shared devotionals, and rare and occasional Masses celebrated by itinerant clergy, some of whom wandered across the countryside with only the most tenuous of ties to a bishop or an established jurisdictional structure. A significant number were footloose French clerics who had fled from the Revolution at home.[14]

Yet by 1870, in contrast, there were four million five-hundred thousand Catholics in the United States, and they formed nearly twelve percent of the nation's population. We may well apply de Tocqueville's reflection on America to the Church in America, that is, "the world learned of her existence and her greatness at one and the same time."

We can describe the origins and growth of the Church in America as three distinct phases. The first, sketched above, was the earliest period of small foundations, isolated communities, and was heavily colored by its European beginnings along with an unconscious view that the unique character of the American Republic imparted to these early communities an openness and flexibility and autonomy in marked contrast to parallel organizations in Europe.

The second phase, from the 1830s and 1840s to the 1870s, witnessed the creation of a national identity. Moreover, an identity clearly associated with the great Irish and German migrations of that period; one group fleeing from famine and oppressive English dominance; the other escaping from the failed revolution in central Europe in the 1840s and the Kulturkampf wars of the 1870s.

For the next one hundred years these two groups would collude to maintain positions of leadership of the Church to the complete exclusion of all other nationalities even when these other groups achieved numerical dominance.

There were three features of this phase that were to mark the rise of Catholicism in America. One, it was an overwhelmingly *urban* event. The great immigrant rushes of the 1840s pushed into the urban centers of the East Coast and the Midwest: Boston, Cincinnati, Chicago, New York, Philadelphia, Milwaukee, and St. Louis became, within one generation, strongholds of the Catholic population.

It did not take long for these immigrants and especially their sons to challenge the political power of the Protestant gentry who had governed the Republic since its origins and certainly earlier. The proliferation of teeming tenements around incipient factories and slaughterhouses represented a sizable voting bloc that was early organized into an informal social service network, and eventually a threat to the governing classes.

The Irish, especially with their long history of surviving and occasionally succeeding in the presence of a paramount power in Ireland, had long developed the skills of maneuver, consolidation, payouts, and paybacks that stood them in good stead in the oily waters of urban politics.

The second feature was the rise of anti-Catholicism as a force in American politics. The increasing visibility of the Catholic population, enhanced by every boat that docked along the East Coast, activated the latent anti-Catholicism of the Protestant majority. "Know-Nothingism" and "Nativism" were forces to be reckoned with in the decades before the Civil War.

Violence against the Church and its people was not unknown, starting with the burning of the Ursuline convent in Boston in 1834; ironically, a place to which the wealthy Protestant leaders of the city sent their daughters for an education! There were intermittent eruptions of burnings and some killings, but by the time of the Civil War this form of anti-Catholicism was in eclipse. It did linger longer throughout the South because of its strong Baptist communities, the reluctance of the new immigrants to move into slaveholding states, and, after the Civil War, the much greater opportunities for personal advancement in the North and the Midwest.

One of the outstanding champions of the Catholic immigrants of this pre–Civil War period was John Hughes, bishop [then the first archbishop (1850)] of New York. Not only did Bishop Hughes threaten to retaliate against anti-Catholic mobs and legislation he demanded that the public schools discontinue the use of the King James Bible in their classrooms since it was a direct challenge to the faith of the Catholic pupils.

The continued heavy Protestant bias of public education impelled Bishop Hughes to argue for, and then establish, the first parochial school system in America. His views were fully endorsed by the national councils of the Church in America held at Baltimore starting in 1852; by the third plenary council in 1884, the bishops *mandated* that every parish in America was to have its own school as a way to avoid the baleful influence of the protestantized public school system.

While anti-Catholicism never really went away in mid-nineteenth-century America, it was attenuated by the heavy participation of Catholics in America in the Union Armies of the Civil War as well as the country's attention being diverted to much more devastating events: the dissolution of the Republic and the struggle over slavery. The drumbeat for freedom, which echoed from the tramp of five-hundred thousand Union soldiers, made anti-Catholicism appear in bad taste if not downright wrong.

The third and perhaps most pervasive and enduring development of the mid-nineteenth-century period for the Catholics in America was the gradual resolution of the tension between those who wished to develop a distinctive American style of Catholicism on this continent and those who were to adhere to the more traditional formularies of the Church in Europe.

The early "americanists" such as Orestes Brownson, Fr. Isaac Hecker, and Bishop John England, the first bishop of Charleston, South Carolina, argued in print and in sermons that the distinctive features of American culture called for a more modern style of Catholicism; one that was more democratic, autonomous, and open to new development of the Spirit.

The greatest champion of this line of thinking was John Ireland, the first archbishop of St. Paul, Minnesota. They argued for the separation of Church and state, the creation of parish councils, had a favorable view of trusteeship in which parishioners ran their own parishes, and trumpeted the proposition that the unique experience of the Church in America offered a great reforming model for the Church throughout the world. They firmly believed that the Church in America—because of its unique environment and cultural and political setting—deserved a level of autonomy and distance from Rome that was not experienced by any other region of the Catholic world.

There were, however, equally compelling leaders who took a more conservative stance and who viewed with concern the developmental theory advanced by the "modernists."

Archbishop Corrigan of New York and Bishop McQuaid of Rochester represented this theme. They were chary about assimilating to a society distinctly Protestant, they nurtured with great tenderness a separate parochial school system, and they argued for a type of insularity for the Church as a "perfect" society parallel to the political society of the state.[15]

Down until the death of Archbishop Ireland in 1918, this division remained public and occasionally acrimonious. In part, ironically, it represented an older, smaller, more fluid constituency against the growing density of the Catholic population who were overwhelmingly conservative and the incremental power of Rome as the organization of the Church matured in America. This view was further strengthened by the wholehearted support of the Jesuits for a more ultramontane stance.

In the 1850s, Rome acknowledged the emergence of the Church in America as one of size and growth. Pius IX multiplied dioceses from Charleston, South Carolina, to Portland, Oregon. By 1870, the original diocese of Baltimore had spawned fifty new dioceses across the country, and there were now six archdioceses in the United States.

As a sign of acceptance of this new community in the universal Church, Pius IX elevated the archbishop of New York, John McCloskey, in 1875 to be the first American cardinal. This was only the beginning of a long lifetime of efflorescence and influence and seemingly irresistible growth. It also represented the eventual triumph—across the board— of the "romanists" over the "americanists," which would culminate in the twentieth century with the Church in America becoming the most *romanophilic* Church in the world with the possible exception of the Church in Ireland.

The third wave of immigration from the 1880s until the First World War brought the kaleidoscope of nationalities to America that were to form the great tsunami of Catholic migration into the United States: Poles, Slovaks, Slovenes, Ukrainian Catholics, Italians, Hungarians, Spaniards, Basques came by the millions to occupy densely populated districts in the large urban centers of the country as well as to fan out as far as the coal mines of Utah, the sheep ranges of Idaho and Nevada, and the fishing vessels of San Francisco.

Their bodies filled the mines, steel mills, factories, shipyards, plains and harbors of the vast industrial and commercial world of late nineteenth-century America. It was the happy convergence of the emergence of the United States as a great industrial power birthed in the heat of an internecine war and the seemingly endless waves of eager and docile workers. Chicago, which started in only 1831, became the largest Polish city in the world.

Within a very short time, there were thirty-three churches in Buffalo alone where Masses were in Polish. In whole sections of Boston and Philadelphia only Italian was spoken. Wherever these immigrants landed, they clustered in shanties near their workplaces and pooled their meager resources to build a Church, which was to be the center of their religious and social life as a ghetto community.

The work was hard, the hours were long, but they had something they could never have found in Naples, Budapest, Krakow, or Bratislava: hope for a better life for their children. Thus were the raw materials in place for the dazzling growth of the Church in the first half of the twentieth century.

It would be mind-numbing to catalog the national growth of the Church in the early twentieth century by chapter and verse. Perhaps an effective way to convey its breathtaking development would be simply to cite one relatively small and remote diocese and the changes made in it under the leadership of one of the many legendary bishops who dotted the early twentieth-century landscape. I cite it as well because it was my introduction to a Catholic culture of which I had not a clue.

What follows as a snapshot of one modest diocese was replicated in dozens of cities of America and in the great urban centers at a magnitude of five and ten times the rate of growth described below.

> With the death of Bishop Fitzmaurice on June 18, 1920, Bishop John Mark Gannon (1920–1996) succeeded to the Erie See. It was the beginning of a golden era in the history of the Erie Diocese. During the forty-six years of Gannon's episcopate the physical expansion and the spiritual development of the diocese was unprecedented. The purchase of the former Metcalf home on West Ninth and Sassafras Street for a bishop's residence began a long series of activities, which facilitated the almost miraculous expansion of Catholic institutions.

> Among the first was the Cathedral Preparatory School for Boys, which Gannon at first envisioned as a seminary. The school opened its doors in September 1921. In 1923, he laid the cornerstone for St. Joseph's Home for Children, a million-

dollar facility that provided housing and care for over three hundred children for several decades. During the first decade of his episcopacy, he also encouraged the foundation of Villa Maria and Mercyhurst Colleges. In 1933, he established Cathedral College, a two-year institution that was the forerunner of Gannon University. Other institutions that were either founded or expanded during Gannon's administration include Spencer Hospital, Meadville; St. Vincent's Hospital, Erie; Andrew Kaul Memorial Hospital, St. Marys; San Rosario, Cambridge Springs; St. Mary's Home, Erie; Harborcreek Training School for Boys, Erie; Gannondale for Girls, Erie; and the Erie Day Nursery, Erie. The litany of construction projects included the establishment of twenty-eight new parishes, the erection of forty-nine new churches, twenty elementary schools, eight parish high schools, five independent high schools administered by the religious communities of women, five diocesan regional high schools which replaced several parish high schools and one seminary.

In the field of religious education, approximately twenty social halls and catechetical centers were constructed. The march of construction also included seven new rectories, five renovated rectories, twelve new convents, two renovated convents, a new Benedictine Motherhouse on East Lake Road in Erie, and the expansion and

renovation of the Motherhouse of the Congregation
of the Divine Spirit. For the first time, too, missions
appeared in the small rural communities of Spring
Center, Sarah Furnace, and Rimersburg.

Indeed, by the time he relinquished the reins of
authority Bishop Gannon could claim that he was
God's bricklayer for forty-eight years in the thirteen
counties of northwestern Pennsylvania.[16]

This catalog of construction and organizational maturation
recurred in every community of America where a sizable
Catholic population existed. It was overseen by a generation
of forceful prelates gifted with excellent management skills.
Cardinal Dougherty in Philadelphia (1918–1951), Cardinal
Mundelein in Chicago (1915–1939), Cardinal O'Connell in
Boston (1907–1944), Cardinal Hayes in New York (1919–1938)
and Cardinal Glennon in Saint Louis (1903–1946) were the
exemplars of the "Bishop/Builder" bestriding their respective
cities as part construction boss and part political force.

The development of the Church was not limited to its
ecclesiastical or parochial growth. From the 1860s forward, a
vast army of women religious communities erected hospitals,
social service agencies, high schools, orphanages, centers for
the poor, and outreaches for the homeless—dozens by the
decades—in practically every city in the nation. Only in some
of the more remote regions of the American South did one find
a community without a Catholic hospital or school.

The sisters followed first the mining frontier and then the
farming frontier across the west. In 1880 alone, for example,

hospitals were erected in Tucson, AZ, Atlanta, GA, Omaha, NE, Astoria, OR, Leadville, CO, and Bloomington, IL. In 1882, eight more hospitals were opened, in 1887, eleven were opened; sixteen in 1900 and twenty-three in 1902. The pace continued decade after decade. In less than a century, dozens of religious communities led by the Sisters of Charity, the Sisters of Mercy, and the Franciscan Sisters had built over eight hundred hospitals in the United States.[17]

In tandem, the same communities staffed the ever-expanding parochial educational system. Seventy-five years after Bishop Hughes of New York set up the first parish school, there were *over ten thousand parish schools* across America, overwhelmingly staffed by women in religious communities, a great number of them indigenous to the Catholic Church in America. So large had been the influx of the Catholic immigrants that even after the age of immigration ended with the Immigration Act of 1924, the fecundity of the Catholic families ensured that the Catholic population would not only increase absolutely but would also increase relative to the other religious denominations in the country. By the turn of the twentieth century, Roman Catholics constituted the single largest religious group in America.

By the end of World War I, the Catholic population of the United States had reached a certain cultural and social status. It was no longer only an immigrant Church; it had become a lower-middle-class and middle-class Church of professionals and semiprofessionals. Sons and daughters of coal workers and ironmongers were business people and storekeepers. More were going to college than ever before and more were entering the religious communities and the priesthood than ever before.

Out of this prosperous cultural scene emerged some significant developments that characterized the first half of the twentieth century. One of these was the rise of organized labor. Their involvement goes back to Cardinal Gibbons' defense of the Knights of Labor in the 1870s, Leo XIII's encyclical on Capital and Labor in 1891 and the seminal work of Fr. John A. Ryan in the first decades of the twentieth century.

There seemed to be a natural affinity between the American pursuit of justice and the Catholic principles of social action. Fr. Ryan played a critical role in the American bishops' document, the *Bishops' Program of Social Reconstruction*, which was substantially his own work. His work on distributive justice sought, on the basis of natural law, to find a third way between individualist capitalism and collectivist socialism. His writings and positions on social and economic issues shaped the tone and emphasis of New Deal rhetoric and policy.[18]

Father Ryan, from his faculty position at Catholic University of America, did much in the early decades of the twentieth century to add intellectual heft to Catholic thought—especially on social issues—and to achieve a public recognition for his work by public figures of both parties of the best thinking in Catholicism on contemporary issues. His stature was enhanced when the American bishops, in 1919, formally established the National Catholic Welfare Council (NCWC) as the public face of the episcopate and appointed Fr. Ryan as head of the Social Action Department of the NCWC.

The second significant development was the emergence of Catholic Action—in the broadest sense—by the rise of the proliferation of social and devotional associations such as the Holy Name Society, the St. Vincent de Paul Society, the Knights of Columbus, the Catholic Daughters, legions of sodalities and confraternities for pious and charitable purpose, the building of over two hundred colleges and universities on top of almost twenty-five hundred high schools. It seemed to have been an astoundingly fortunate melding of Roman Catholicism and American democracy in the process of which the immigrant Catholics embraced assimilation to American culture with the zeal of the convert.

Concomitantly, the warp and woof of Catholic culture in the United States took on a distinctively American cast that seemed to bypass all of the intractable conflicts and tragedies that so marked Catholic Christianity in the old world. This new mythic understanding of Catholicism in the modern world with a recognizable American hue was to be most eloquently adumbrated by the celebrated civil theologian, Fr. John Courtney Murray, S.J., in *We Hold These Truths*, his seminal work on the relationship of the Faith to the American proposition. In a sense, with the *Declaration on Religious Freedom* at the Second Council, the "americanists" reasserted their dominance over the "romanists" and, indeed, projected it to the Universal Church.

As the Catholic community approached the midpoint of the twentieth century, who could gainsay a pervasive sense of confidence, indeed, of triumph? The sons and daughters of coal miners and steelworkers had become teachers, accountants, attorneys, hospital administrators, bishops, abbesses, businessmen, and physicians. They had more than pledged their fealty to the American way of life; they had enthusiastically embraced it as their own. In depression and war they had demonstrated their unstinting loyalty to the Republic and, thus, allayed the not-always-latent anti-Catholicism of the Protestant majority.

Indeed, in the aftermath of war as the threat of communism became real, Roman Catholicism's long- standing criticism and implacable opposition to it strengthened its bond with the larger American society. It seemed that nothing lay before Catholics in America but the broad uplands of prosperity, a stable social order, and a confident Church enjoying one of its millennium-rare occasions of status, success, and prestige.

Yet within a decade, a social hurricane of political and ecclesiastical calamities would wipe away the trust and treasure of generations, dissolve thousands of religious ties, and trigger an exodus of massive proportions by those very persons whose dedication and service sustained the entire edifice of Catholic culture and all its myriad institutions.

IV

Squandering the Legacy:
Anatomy of Decline

"And the last temptation is the greatest treason:
To do the right thing for the wrong reason."
T. S. Eliot

If the legions of immigrant families of the first half of the twentieth century were ever to return, they would hardly recognize the Church that they had so arduously built and in which all of the vital moments of their lives from baptism to interment had taken place. The reasons for the collapse of the historic immigrant Church in America were as devastating as they were unexpected although there were signs for those who could read them that all was not well behind the imposing façade of power and serenity, the regiments of devotions, the bulging convents and crowded seminaries, the massive communion breakfasts, and the hundreds of rituals, litanies, and public events that conveyed permanence, stolidity, stasis, and an indefinite ascendancy.

To understand the collapse of Catholic culture in the United States in the second half of the twentieth century, it is helpful to start with two sets of comparative numbers concerning salient features of the Church in America.

Category	1965	2008
Total population	45,640,619	67,515,016
Cardinals	6	16
Archbishops	29	36
Bishops	212	428
Priests	58,632	42,307
Brothers	12,271	5,095
Sisters	209,000	64,877
Seminarians	48,792	5,180
Parishes	17,088	19,844
Elementary students	4,566,809	1,724,761
High Schools	2,455	1,350
High School Students	1,095,519	672,426
Hospitals	808	556
Patients	16,571,548	84,736,305

* * *

To quote from Stewart's book on the history of American sisters and nuns as they appeared at the end of the 1950s, "These statistics demonstrate the awesome magnitude of the Church. In less than two hundred years, it had grown from a tiny, fragile institution to the largest and most powerful religious denomination in the nation and one of the strongest national Churches in the world."[19]

In the forty years since its apogee, however, the Church has simultaneously expanded in some aspects of its institutional life (overall population and number of dioceses) and severely contracted in its personnel and the breadth of its educational services (numbers of priests, brothers, sisters and students in elementary and high schools). More fundamentally, it has virtually abandoned all the features of its older cultural forms and become a fragmented, uncertain voice besmirched by scandal, flouted by politicians even of the same religion, and institutionally flaccid and benumbed.

Most fatefully of all, the numbers for the current year are by no means stable. The actuarial tables and the infrequency of recruiting new members to established religious communities clearly demonstrate that the number of religious men and women could within a lifetime approach zero.

Let us turn now to some of those reasons for the decline of so imposing an edifice. Many of these reasons were (and are) strongly interrelated so that once a breach, so to speak, occurred in one section of the architecture it would—in domino effect—precipitate a further rupture which would accelerate the decline until the spirit of the entire pile collapsed leaving vast empty structures forlorn in their desuetude and managed by an ever-aging, shrinking, and uncertain community of religious men and women.

Nor can we identify any hierarchy of causes since for some communities one cause was devastating while for others an altogether different factor intervened. At best, we can give a general summary of what were the realities at work that changed the Catholic world in America between 1960 and 1980.

One reason would be as old as religious life itself; that is, the contrast between what Wittberg calls "virtuoso" religiosity and mass religiosity; those who enter religious life for right reasons as opposed to those who enter religious life only for good reasons. It makes all the difference in the world. The virtuosi are those who catch the initial grace to draw closer in a special relationship to Christ and see that that can be done by some particular activity.[20]

A familiar example would be Mother Teresa of Calcutta. Whenever possible, she would reinforce the idea that the purpose of the Missionaries of Charity was *not* to take care of the poor, the abandoned, or the ill. The purpose was to establish and sustain a personal relationship with Christ and that this was done by seeing Christ in the poor, the abandoned, and the ill.

It is the heroic or virtuoso religiosity that creates a fire of grace, that draws new recruits who wish to give themselves to something greater, such as marked the first men who gathered around St. Francis, or the first women who were attracted to the austere life of the Discalced Carmelites established by St. Teresa, or the young men who came to La Trappe in the early eighteenth century and joined de Rancé in shattering the windows of the abandoned monastery on a cold and snowy night to deepen the penance of monks of the strict observance.

In time emerges the *organizational* problem. St. Bernard gave a clear account of it in the twelfth century. The blossoming of the medieval Church, most notably by the widespread growth of the Cistercian Order throughout all of Europe and the increased complexity of the organizational life of the Church, attained a point where confusion and disorder threatened fatally to end the work that was growing so beneficently.

Dealing with zealous postulants clamoring to enter, organizing increasingly more distant establishments, adjudicating legal disputes with secular and even other ecclesiastical authorities, arbitrating internal controversies, all these eventually endangered the great work afoot. St. Bernard says then what happens is that, for the most plausible reasons, it becomes necessary to select leaders who have the skill to "manage the enterprise" for the viability of the whole. Ineluctably, he says, the organization will come to be dominated by its managers and not by its virtuosi, to use Wittberg's term.

A generation of leaders will emerge who are more intent on the governance of the community than in furthering the initial goals for which the community was established. The seeds of eventual decline will have been planted in the full summer of waxing power.

In the short run, it seems to be working as intended: better management increases numbers and multiplies agencies and institutions; all seems to be working as planned. It is telling that at the so-called apogee of the medieval Church, putatively during the pontificate of Innocent III (1198–1216), this organizational rhythm played out as St. Bernard's insight demonstrated. Hardly any of the popes before Innocent III were canon lawyers; after him, hardly any were not.

The institution had become too complex to be governed by sanctity alone. There needed to be rules, and where there are rules, there are men and women adept at managing the rules, and thus the institution. In time, the focus of all the institutional energies is on maintaining the institutional apparatuses—not on what is its informing principle.

In a similar manner, the organic morphing of the institutional life of the Church silently took place in the United States. Even before the summertime of the Church in America, the organization of the Church underwent a profound alternation… and for understandable reasons, and this change was most profound and noticeable in the emergence of new types of bishops.

Many of the mid-century bishops, often drawn from the Irish peasant class, were long on assimilation to the larger American culture, eager to stay below the radar, and of generally a pious and uncontentious nature. This "prophetic" or "pastoral" episcopacy turned into the "managerial" episcopacy. This silent transformation can best be illuminated in summary form in the careers of four prominent relates of the twentieth century.

William Cardinal O'Connell became archbishop of Boston in 1907 and was raised to the cardinalate in 1911, the first of the Boston archbishops so named. He remained in that position until his death in 1944.[21]

Both accomplishments attained with no little indeorous finagling with influential friends in Rome where, serving a stint as rector of the Pontifical North American College, he shamelessly curried the favor of the powerful secretary of state, Rafael Merry Del Val, who was instrumental in securing for O'Connell first, the diocese of Portland, Maine, and then the Archdiocese of Boston. In lusting after both positions, he was not above libeling his predecessors and besmirching the reputations of other prelates in contention for those sees.

Moreover, he was firmly in the camp of the *romanists* and unashamedly used his explicit loyalty to Rome against the *americanist* ideas of men such as Archbishop Ireland to advance his own cause. In 1918 when Cardinal Farley of New York died, O'Connell made an ostentatious tour of the Archdiocese of New York to promote his own candidacy. However, for once, the Irish clerical "mafia" in the New York Archdiocese served a good purpose in stifling his embarrassing efforts.

In addition to a poorly disguised ambition for power and authority and a positive gift for malfeasance, he brought to his office an outstanding set of managerial skills. He was a gifted administrator and was perhaps the first prelate of the Church in America to insist on effective and comprehensive business practices in the management of the affairs of the Church. He centralized the administration of the archdiocese and rationalized its funding operations. He insisted on full accountability and disciplined finance. For two full generations, he ordained dozens of priests each year, dramatically expanded the number of parishes to over two hundred, and created a regional complex of elementary and secondary educational institutions without peer in the nation.

He witnessed—and reveled in—the decline of the puritan gentry in the politics of Boston and in Massachusetts. He wielded such pervasive power in his thirty-three years that he had a virtual veto on all public policy issues in the city. When he took to task the legendary Irish mayor of Boston, James Michael Curley, for alleged dishonesty, the voters of Boston refused to reelect him as mayor.

But his successes came at a price. His penchant for frequent ocean cruises earned him the nickname of *gangplank Bill*; his winter home in the Bahamas offered him a comfortable retreat from the harsh Boston winters.

His priest-nephew, as chancellor of the archdiocese, maintained a not-so-discreet liaison with a woman in New York to whom he was allegedly married; he paid out thousands of dollars to hush up some of the more disreputable behaviors of another young priest (with whom he lived) who was the editor of the diocesan newspaper and who was also married.[22]

He seldom said Mass, paraded around Boston in his custom-made Pierce-Arrow, and had an impressive cellar of fine wines. He was not only a cheat and a crook; he was also a liar. Only at the end of the last century were forgeries uncovered in which the cardinal attempted to pad his autobiography so as to enhance his image. As Charles Morris recounts about Cardinal O'Connell, "A dreadful human being and a bad priest, he was undeniably a successful cardinal."[23]

Dennis Joseph Cardinal Dougherty became archbishop of Philadelphia in 1915 and received his red hat in 1921. While completing his studies in Rome, he became acquainted with a number of movers and shakers in the curial bureaucracy including Merry Del Val and Cardinal Gasparri, then secretary of state, who would be instrumental in advancing his career. He came to the attention of the Vatican when he was taken from his position at St. Joseph's Seminary in Philadelphia and was asked to serve as bishop of the Philippines in the wake of the American conquest of that archipelago as a result of the Spanish-American War and the suppression of the Aguinaldo insurrection of 1899–1901.

He took a flaccid and corrupt Church and by draconian measures, wholesale cashiering and meticulous attention to designing effective organizational structures, and an uncanny sense of personnel selection, he turned it into a vibrant ecclesial community. His successes in this endeavor revealed his strengths… and his weaknesses: a commanding presence, a capacious memory for myriad details, an excellent judge of men, an untroubled self-confidence, great organizational skills, an overweening style of micromanaging, a firm belief that encouraging words for a job well done induced complacency and laziness, and a truculence that brooked no challenges from anyone.

When his tenure was complete, he was rewarded with the bishopric of Buffalo with the promise that the next major archdiocese to become vacant would become his. Fortuitously for his own interest, Philadelphia was available in 1915. He governed the archdiocese until his death in 1951.

Like his fellow cardinal in Boston, Cardinal Dougherty was a master builder; in fact, he called himself "God's bricklayer." He developed a remarkable real estate sense and religiously trolled through the expanding suburbs of Philadelphia buying up property in the path of future expansion. He would hold property for years, renting it back to its former owners, until it was time to build the *de rigueur* parish plant: church, rectory, school, convent. He would loan the parish money for this construction and then sell off the remaining land almost always for a handsome profit.

Startlingly at the end of his tenure, Philadelphia was the only diocese in America with no debt and over seven-hundred million dollars in the bank. Schools and parishes mushroomed throughout the metropolitan area, culminating in the erection of the largest high school in the world, Cardinal Dougherty High School, of course. His managerial acumen was such that for each of the thirty years of his rule, he was able to forward to Rome one million dollars per annum as a "contribution" to the work of the Church universal. Needless to say, he suffered no interference from the Vatican during his long reign; for obvious reasons, he was called *romanissimus*, the most "roman" of the American ecclesiastics.

He ruled the 1,000+ priests of his archdiocese with the charm of a plantation overseer and the warmth of a maximum security prison warden. It is likely that his gruff, bullying, and ever-demanding style drove his superintendent of schools, Msgr. John Bonner—a remarkable man who oversaw 328 institutions with one assistant—to a premature death by heart attack at the age of fifty-five.[24]

Anyone who demurred at a decision would swiftly find himself exiled to a remote and poverty-stricken parish of immigrant coal miners. Anyone with a drinking problem was sent to a retreat house to dry out—no questions asked—and any priest with a sexual problem was summarily dismissed and exiled from the archdiocese forthwith, accompanied by a kind of paper trail mark-of-Cain, lest he try to secure a position elsewhere.

He demanded to know every detail in the countless parishes and schools of his archdiocese and insisted on making every decision even to the color of the drapes in a convent or the choices of desks in a given school. He levied burdensome "tithing" on all the parishes of the archdiocese and hounded every pastor to make his annual block collection in his parish. The priests of the archdiocese were the most poorly paid priests in America.

However, he was not above sharing in the bounty of his archdiocese since he spent his annual one- or two-month-long vacation in the South of France in exceedingly comfortable circumstances while the operations of the archdiocese hummed along building buildings and collecting assessments. Like his compatriot Cardinal O'Connell to the north, he also enjoyed extended Caribbean cruises, usually with a bevy of his sisters' families on whom he touchingly doted.

In the depths of the Depression (1936), he purchased *The Terraces* for $115,000 to serve as his official residence and proceeded to spend an additional $100,000 for "improvements." When he returned from his transatlantic vacations, he expected special consideration upon landing in New York and insisted on having his limousine waiting for him.

George Cardinal Mundelein, though born in New York City where he rose to be auxiliary bishop of Brooklyn, made his name in Chicago when he became the archbishop of that city in 1915. He was made a cardinal in 1924 and governed the archdiocese until his death in 1939. Cut from the same bolt as his colleagues in Boston and Philadelphia, he evinced a different but pervasive strain of the development of the Church in America: its "Irishness," even though he came from immigrant German stock.

The city over which he was appointed archbishop had grown to be the great heartland metropolis of the nation, the nexus of a great national railroad system, the cynosure of a national meatpacking empire, the trade and mercantile emporium of the Mississippi Valley, and the home of the most diverse elements of ethnic Catholics in America, the most prominent of which were the Polish followed closely by the Italians, the Slovaks, the Slovenes, the Czechs, and the Uniate Ukrainians.

In the absence of strong episcopal leadership in the nineteenth century, the Church in the Archdiocese of Chicago (made an archdiocese in 1880) were congeries of "national" parishes where active boards of laymen ensured that serving pastors were of the same ethnic origin as the parishioners.

Territoriality—geographically defined parish lines—was an alien concept to many Chicago Catholics.

It also was rightly suspected as a strategy to subject the national parishes to ecclesiastical centralization. It was also in Chicago that some features of "trusteeism" flourished long after it had faded away in other areas of strong episcopal control and had been proscribed by the papacy and outlawed in the Third Plenary Council of Baltimore in 1884.[25]

The ethnic character of the Church in Chicago was perhaps more pronounced than it was in any of the major metropolitan areas of the Church in America with a parish and its parishioners worshipping on one corner having little or nothing to do with either of the comparable parishes on the other corners of the same intersection because they were of a different nationality. The ethnic minorities who constituted these national Churches fought vigorously to maintain their identities and distinctiveness. It was Cardinal Mundelein's task to redesign these components into a modern Catholic archdiocese.

He fought a relentless war against the national churches, drove out the trustee concept, and unilaterally absorbed the national churches into the archdiocesan framework. Armed with a burgeoning crop of Irish priests, he ran roughshod over ethnic sensibilities and compelled the Catholic minorities to accept the Irish domination of parish life, along with all of the strictures and culture that came from an Irish Church.

The Poles, who outnumbered the Irish, fought desperately against the consolidation and pled earnestly for the appointment of a Polish bishop as an auxiliary, a request that the cardinal, with equal vigor, quashed. Battalions of Irish nuns and Irish pastors flogged the ethnic minorities to adopt, albeit without much enthusiasm, the habits and mores of early twentieth-century Irish Catholicism, a heady mixture of saccharine piety, prissy moralisms, and bare-knuckle enforcement practices.

By the end of his episcopacy, Cardinal Mundelein had managed to reconstitute the archdiocese. While less than twenty percent of the Catholics in the archdiocese were Irish, a third of the parishes were staffed by Irish priests, most of the schools were staffed by Irish nuns, and half of the auxiliary bishops of Chicago were Irish. The freebooting, wild diversity of the later nineteenth-century national parishes was transformed into the stereotypical Irish-American Church of the first half of the twentieth century.

He mirrored as well the building boom of his contemporary prelates and that coupled with the mass migrations of Catholic ethnics into the area helped the Archdiocese of Chicago to became the largest Catholic episcopal unit in the world. He inaugurated the practice of financing parish and school expansions through "Bishop Bonds" and worked with Chicago financial power brokers to underwrite massive construction loans and projects.

So influential was he that a mere mention of the need for a consultation would bring bankers a-running to the episcopal offices. He built one of the most beautiful and elaborate seminaries in the country, St. Mary of the Lake/Mundelein Seminary, on a thousand acres of land to the northwest of the city.

He was as politically active in Chicago as Cardinal O'Connell had been in Boston. Moreover, he was an ardent proponent of the New Deal and played no small part in assuring that Chicago remained a Democratic Party stronghold throughout the 1930s and beyond. He and President Roosevelt were on a first-name basis and he did more than perhaps any other prelate in America to solidify the ties between the vast number of working-class Catholics and the Democratic Party. Perhaps even more than in Boston, Chicago evidenced the solid ties between Irish urban politics and ecclesiastical power that, with occasional stresses, perdures to the present day.

Francis Cardinal McIntyre made his name as a highly successful stock trader in New York working at the New York Stock Exchange (NYSE), becoming the manager of a successful brokerage house at an early age. However, when he was twenty-nine years old, he turned his back on Wall Street and finance and became a priest. His administrative talents were hard to hide, and quickly he rose to be chancellor of the Archdiocese of New York, serving as Cardinal Spellman's right-hand man.

After a number of highly successful administrative appointments, he was made archbishop of Los Angeles in 1948 (on the recommendation of Cardinal Spellman who by virtue of his close friendship with Pius XII maintained a choke hold on episcopal appointments in the United States) and became a cardinal in 1953. As with those prelates of a previous generation, his career vectored into the age of the expansion of Los Angeles into a great metropolis. His staunch conservative outlook and fierce business acumen fitted perfectly with the prevailing Protestant culture of Southern California.

He became, in fact, the metropolitan of the west and the first cardinal in that region of the country.

Also like his predecessors in eastern archdioceses, he was an ardent builder. It was said that a parish school opened every 151 days in the Archdiocese of Los Angeles while he was primate. Like Cardinal Dougherty, he had a nose for real estate and bought far and wide in an ever-rising real estate market. In time, the Archdiocese of Los Angeles was to rival and then surpass Chicago as the largest diocese in America (it still is).

Perhaps no archdiocese of America typified the plastic optimism, white middle-class culture, and treacly materialism of America of the 1950s as Los Angeles. Boosterism and religiosity became natural bedfellows in what appeared to be an unparalleled success story of growth, Irish bonhomie, and hard business sense. The Pat O'Brien-Loretta Young-Barry Fitzgerald evocation of bathetic Irish religious sentimentality, unrefined reactionary politics, and dime novel-type religious stories and movies (reaching its embarrassing nadir in 1945 with the Oscar-winning *The Bells of Saint Mary's*) enjoyed an envied niche in Southern California folklore.

In contrast, the 1977 novel *True Confessions* by John Gregory Dunne, the screenplay for which was written by his wife, Joan Didion, is a barely fictional account of the seamier side of Southern California Catholicism in the 1940s and 1950s.

Yet Cardinal McIntyre became increasingly rigid as his tenure unfolded. Like Cardinal Spellman in New York, he strenuously resisted the liturgical reforms of the Second Vatican Council until directly commanded to implement them by the Holy See.

The rising tide of Hispanic migration, which was to come to dominate the Church in Los Angeles, was first a discomfort and then a disturbance which he then construed into defiance. He handled the importunities of the Hispanic community badly, refusing to recognize their just grievances.

His insensitivity to Hispanics mirrored Cardinal Mundelein's toward the Polish: both minority groups were sedulously barred from any share of ecclesial power, which was kept firmly in the hands of the Irish clergy. He exiled to bleak desert parishes socially activist priests who were becoming uncomfortably vocal and he became an ardent defender of the establishment in the disturbances of the 1960s that were tearing his city apart.

He became more authoritarian and spent the closing years of his reign in an unedifying and protracted conflict with the Sisters of the Immaculate Heart of Mary, who, in their defense, were implementing the reforms recommended by the Vatican Council. His response was to dismiss all of them immediately from the myriad teaching positions they held in the archdiocese. Compelled to retire by the Vatican in 1970 at the age of eighty-four, he died a broken man in retirement and obscurity at the age of ninety-three.[26]

These brief synopses of four powerful prelates evidence the crises and conflicts that bedeviled the Church in America. Nor are they isolated cases of idiosyncratic uses of power. They, in fact, became the "models of success" to which brother archbishops and bishops aspired. In each case, their success was legitimated by the bestowal of the red hat—the enviable ticket of entrée to the most select body in the Catholic Church.

As the structures became more formidable and elaborate, their prowess and power intensified. Yet none of them (or their emulators) could reasonably be singled out as models of personal holiness or paladins of profound personal transformation into the imitation of Christ. Their piety was conventional; their vision was tunneled; their administrative style was autocratic.

They, in fact, bear a serious responsibility for that culture of the priesthood that was to be clothed in uncommon shame in the sexual scandals that stained the Church in the 1960s and 1970s. They failed to anneal their priests in the most fundamental prerequisite of their vocation—to be Christ to their parishioners—in great part because they, themselves, failed to be Christs for their archdioceses. They were eminently successful in managing problems... in the short run; they were failures in being Christ-like in *forestalling* problems.

Yet as St. Bernard grievously noted, it was as natural as the rising of the sun that these men would wield the power they did and be the kind of prelates they were.

The rise of the leaders of the immigrant Church in one long generation from steerage to palaces of power was reared on some presuppositions that proved to be less than durable:

(a) that the Mass of the Catholic laity would be stable, unitary, and docile;

(b) that the methods, rhythms, and mores of the Catholic life would perdure as they existed into the foreseeable future;

(c) that the public persona of the Catholic priest and Catholic sister would remain unchanged and that the social status of those personae would not be tarnished;

(d) that the nexus between Irish urban elites and ecclesiastical power would remain unchallenged;

(e) that the inherent promise of America for social and economic mobility would not lure the Catholic faithful out of their current status with only limited career choices,

(f) that episcopal power could be wielded without accountability,

(g) that elementary and secondary education as well as health care would remain personal, easily accessible, and cheap.

Yet all these assumptions vaporized in the heady turmoil of the 1960s and 1970s. And as they did, the massive institutional structures hardened and became brittle all the while obscuring rumbles of discontent, flabby moral behavior, lifeless and mechanical processes of formation, and the alienation of potential religious who would have served as the virtuosi of the next generation of the Church in America.

The great network of institutions lasted barely two generations when it was rip-sawed by changes of a tectonic scope. The Catholic colleges and universities declared their independence, the Second Vatican Council signaled the end of the Tridentine Church (the traditional Latin Mass), the sons and daughters of the immigrants moved into the professions and out to the suburbs, and the prince-bishops who governed the Church in America found their writ increasingly faltering, challenged, and ignored.

The development of Medicare and Medicaid transformed how health care was to be delivered in the United States and required serious organizational adaptation on the part of the 800+ health facilities staffed by religious women in the country.

The saccharine portrayals of priests and nuns as played by Bing Crosby and Ingrid Bergman in *The Bells of Saint Mary's* lasted no longer than an overdose of sentimentality should. By the 1960s, the diminishment of this pseudo-idealized version was accelerated by countless personal and real experiences by Catholic students of tyrannical nuns, leering clerics, and increasingly neurotic brothers and sisters in the classroom who hardly inspired emulation. The idealized versions of all things

Catholic that had matured in the 1930s and 1940s became increasingly at variance with the lived experience of millions of Catholics who grew, year by year, increasingly different from their immigrant ancestors.

The generation of bishops and archbishops of the period 1970–2010 have been engaged in a massive fire sale of consolidation, liquidation, and damage control. The vast educational systems that had been created continue to shrink. The great networks of parishes continue to be fused or closed. The healthcare networks have been consolidated into massive—and costly—systems, increasingly detached from the religious spirit which attended their origins regardless of the complacent mission statements to the contrary. The battalions of men and women who staffed all those institutions continue to be fewer and older.

As one looks over the current landscape that the titans of the early twentieth-century Church created in America at the meridian of their power, the words of Shelley's poem, "Ozymandias", may readily come to mind:

> I met a traveller from an antique land
> Who said: Two vast and trunkless legs of stone
> Stand in the desert. Near them on the sand,
> Half sunk, a shatter'd visage lies, whose frown
> And wrinkled lip and sneer of cold command
> Tell that its sculptor well those passions read
> Which yet survive, stamp'd on these lifeless things,
> The hand that mock'd them and the heart that fed.
> And on the pedestal these words appear:
> 'My name is Ozymandias, king of kings:

Look on my works, ye Mighty, and despair!'
Nothing beside remains: round the decay
Of that colossal wreck, boundless and bare,
The lone and level sands stretch far away.

Another significant cause of the decline was the massive dislocation of the members of the religious orders, and, in a parallel fashion, the shrinkage of the priesthood. By the mid-1950s, the religious communities that had been so effective throughout the latter part of the nineteenth century and the first part of the twentieth century in creating the Church in America had pretty much banked their religious zeal and had become overwhelmingly populated by those who entered religious life for good reasons but not for right reasons.

And the good reasons were persuasive: emulating a teacher who had a profound influence on one's formation, a desire to make a contribution, an eagerness to alleviate pain and suffering, a commitment to push back the black curtain of ignorance and prejudice, or to follow in the footsteps of a pious aunt or uncle (or two or three pious aunts or uncles) who had chosen religious life.

Then there were other, and not as good, reasons: a desire to avoid the risks of the world or to leave one tightly knit family for another, an easier path for ambition than the world offered, an aversion to disappoint a father or mother who had their heart set on a (or some) vocation(s) in the family, an escape from an oppressive family environment, and hundreds of other reasons buried in the hearts of those thousands of men and women who entered religious life in the 1940s and 1950s naively, uncritically, and with the touching belief that the world would never change.

Externally, all seemed on the right trajectory. Parochial schools were still being opened with numbing frequency, hospitals were still being built, social services were still being expanded, and the novitiates were still adding wings for new recruits. The vast institutional framework seemed to be humming along beautifully.

Interestingly, not everyone was satisfied with this state of things. And as often happens, it was the papacy that began to call for change. As early as 1950, Pius XII issued a series of allocutions to religious congregations to develop more flexibility and discard what was unessential to the performance of their respective apostolates. He called for "a renewal of the primitive spirit of the congregation and an adaptation of that spirit to present-day needs" as well as to enhance the educational skills and formation of religious women.[27]

He went so far as to establish the *Regina Mundi Institute* in Rome in 1956 for this very purpose. This was to be but the overture of the symphony of demand for wholesale reform that was to come.

When in the late 1960s, these serried battalions of workers in the Lord's field were directed by new currents in the Church emanating out of the Second Vatican Council to engage in *ressourcement* on a profound level, to reseize the genius of their respective founders and foundresses, to rekindle the flame that brought them into existence in the first place, to rededicate themselves to that grace and fire that drove their originators to heroic levels of action, they were shocked; some, even to disbelief. The whole cardboard world of elaborate wimples, meticulous rules, conventional expectations, unchanging hours, and the absence of challenge and risk came crashing down around them.[28]

For some, it was liberation, and they fled back into the world mildly exhilarated… and fearful. For others, claiming to find a "voice," they started jettisoning everything that was associated with the historic character of their specific community, and after they had stripped it with Presbyterian thoroughness, they themselves took to the exits leaving wreckage for those who stayed behind. For yet others, it was as if the scales had fallen from their eyes and they saw the world in which they had lived—for some, a good quarter century of their lives— as self-serving, institutionally sclerotic, edifice fixated, and ignorant of the pressing needs of a wounded world.[29]

While it is not true in any sociologically rigorous and methodical way, by and large, those who bolted in largest numbers from their respective communities were more "people-minded" while those who chose to stay were more "institutional-minded." The former often went off to become social workers, community organizers, advocates for the alleviation of poverty and marginalization, or members of organizations that dealt with missions in some direct or indirect way.

The latter rose to positions of authority in managing their various whipsawed communities through the swirling rapids of change, dislocation, and contraction. They negotiated the closing of schools, the merging of hospitals, the shuttering of convents, and the physical well-being of an ever-aging population of compatriots.

The storms of contraction also had psychological and negative consequences. It corrosively ate away the sense of cohesion and community. Religious communities fragmented into satellite pods of threes and fours leaving the fortress-like convent, that once housed dozens of active, contributing men and women, to morph into retirement home-cum-infirmary for the increasingly growing number of aged members of the community.

The contraction environment further enervated the communities by less committed recruitment. Since it was hard to say what the community's purpose was (a lack of "role clarity" as Wittberg calls it), it was hard to inspire anyone to join it. In addition, some communities formally discouraged young women from joining, exuding an aura of decline, dispiritedness, and inexorable dissolution; hardly a climate to excite the high hopes of idealistic or religiously realistic women.

Now came the reckoning for those decades of lifeless formation and conventional behaviors, of the superficial reliance on doubtful assumptions about life in the Church as well as in the world. There were no great spiritual resources upon which to draw. The religious materials for the formation of a Christ-centered life were denatured derivatives of the great texts of the seventeenth and eighteenth centuries or even earlier.

Hollow at the core now, the spirit of renewal to which the Church called all these people prompted a gaggle of increasingly bizarre activities. New Age nostrums, experimental psychological inventories, whole processes of discernment with increasingly murky goals, and dozens of other panaceas were trotted out to fill the void, but none could replenish the pool of spiritual wealth nor stanch the hemorrhage of departures.

In some cases, communities voluntarily jettisoned their institutional responsibilities by cutting schools and hospitals loose from the grounds of their origins. While an edifying gesture to reconceptualize a new apostolate for the community (usually to serve the poor or address similar social needs), it was the height of irresponsibility insofar as these now "autonomous" institutions—be they schools or hospitals or social service agencies—were left to confront ever more costly challenges with ever fewer resources. It also severed the connections to what historically had been the most promising arena of recruiting new members to the parent community.

The larger culture played a role as well. The heady liberation of the 1960s and early 1970s in the larger American life, including incipient feminism, had the effect of juxtaposing the new against the old, the hip against the passé, the free against the controlled, the *au courant* against the stick-in-the-mud.

As always in history, it was a lopsided battle and the forces of the future carried the day. The genteel nihilism of the generation of the 1960s tore through the ranks of men's and women's religious orders no less devastatingly than it did through millions of middle-class homes across the country.

For many, it was the rationale for departure. For what turned out to be the more destructive, it signaled the wholesale change in the life of the religious community. New formularies of practice and prayer followed each other with bewildering frequency until, in sheer exhaustion, some irenic forms that somehow accommodated a diverging range of views about one's personal spiritual life without much focus or clarity were embraced.

A third factor was the dramatic contraction of resources. The religious communities of the 1960s, beset by all of the turmoil of the times as well as significant changes in the environment in which they flourished, set in motion an ineluctable series of dominoes that once triggered accelerated a painful diminishment of resources.

As the certitudes fell away about the value and focus of religious life, its attractiveness ebbed drastically. Women communities, especially, were either unable or as often unwilling to recruit new candidates because of the uncertainties of their very purpose. Simultaneously, for young women ever-increasing career opportunities opened before them.

The continual decline of the status of religious life served as another disincentive. The emerging caricature of nuns as immature, neurotic, over-sheltered, or worse, hardly inspired young women to take a religious life seriously.

A further unintended consequence of the jettisoning of their institutions was that, where formerly there were many opportunities for women to develop strong leadership skills in managing large healthcare facilities or complex colleges and schools, these options disappeared in the changing environment in which education and health care existed in the second half of the twentieth century.

The general support of the laity shriveled as the features of parochial education, for example, became increasingly bimodal: large, wealthy, suburban parishes and high schools which did not need support, or poor, inner-city schools with largely non-Catholic populations which could not get support.

A critical type of resource that was irretrievably lost was the delicate balance between the episcopacy and the women religious communities that had been a source of creative tension in the days of the immigrant Church. As the religious communities undergoing contraction took up various blends of feminism, it exacerbated the natural tension between the two.

The irony was that they became more strident as they became less powerful. In an earlier day, women religious could face down a pushy bishop or cardinal by arraying a powerful combination of institutional power and sheer numbers. Every bishop knew how critically he depended on the work of the nuns and what were the limits of his power vis-à-vis the sisters. The religious head of a hospital staffed by dozens of sisters could not be easily intimidated.

The late nineteenth century and early twentieth century is replete with stories of celebrated rows between bishops and nuns. Most of which ended up in Mexican standoffs. It is inconceivable to imagine something like that happening in the last thirty years.

Another equally important reason for the decline has nothing to do with the internal logic of institutional fabric, nor the parlous state of religious formation, nor the arrogance of episcopal power, nor the cross currents of ordinary cultural change. It had and has to do with the particular "exceptionalism" of the Church in America in the twentieth century.

It is especially critical to understand this because a failure to do so prompts all kinds of musings as to how to revive the religious orders, or concomitantly, announce that the rebirth of religious life is an illusion since the means and methods used for the development of religious life for nineteen hundred years have irretrievably been lost. To assert the latter is to condemn oneself to determinism about personal reform and religious life that would have no explanation for the recurring revivals and reforms in the history of the Church.

The Church in America in the late nineteenth and early twentieth centuries was exceptional because it was shaped by a peculiar set of historical circumstances that were unique. The environmental factors which gave rise to it were as distinctive as those that prompted the efflorescence of the Cistercian monasteries in the eleventh and twelfth centuries.

The classic age of American Catholicity was the happy confluence of a number of astoundingly favorable—and unrelated—events. Among the most salient would be the following:

(a) the benign neglect of a national government which publicly confessed incompetence to interfere in any of the internal affairs of the Church and nationally believed in a public venue of maximum freedom where each person was assured the right to swim… or sink on their own;

(b) the massive immigration—starting with the Irish and the Germans in the 1840s and 1850s—of millions of Roman Catholics until the turn of the twentieth century who were overwhelmingly uneducated, unskilled, and friendless. They, therefore, found the church, the school, and the ethnic community the social mechanisms for tools for survival, stability, and the future;

(c) the unchallenged supremacy of one ethnic group— the Irish—who seized the reins of ecclesiastical power and tenaciously held onto them by means foul as well as fair and in happy collusion with a generation of powerful Irish urban "bosses" whose fundamental political principle was "to take care of one's own";

(d) the hostile—and until the mid-twentieth century— prevailing Protestant culture which in a thousand ways exploited, marginalized, barred, and retarded the Catholic peoples in preventing them access to the economic and social benefits of American citizenship and unwittingly giving them, at the same time, a remarkable and almost unheard of cohesiveness. This had the effect of driving millions of young men and women into avenues that offered opportunity for success, careers of social cachet, and an extension of the closely knit social community from which they arose: the priesthood and the religious life;

(e) the apogee of the Catholic Revival of the nineteenth century which arose in France and found its greatest opportunity for growth and expansion in the enormous educational and healthcare needs of the Catholic communities in the United States;

(f) the coincidental rise of the United States as a great economic and world power which infused the nation with a rising tide of wealth and prosperity, and on the principal that "a rising tide lifts all boats," the Catholic population saw their most cherished dreams realized in two generations. Those billions of dollars permitted the rearing of those massive institutional structures of the Church, sent their children to college and into the professions, funded the national healthcare system wherein they were taken care of by regiments of religious women and buried by a squad of priests, one or more of whom might be a son or nephew.

It is impossible to overstress the importance of these socioeconomic and political reasons in not *creating* the Church in America but in *shaping* the kind of Church it became. By the turn of the twenty-first century, *every one* of these presuppositions had been either overcome, repudiated, or been bypassed by historical events.

But every eventide is followed, eventually, by a dawn. So it is with the Church.

Out of the flotsam and jetsam of the collapse of the classical world, the first blooms of the Benedictine Order sprouted on a remote mountain in central Italy. Even before the Napoleonic Wars laid waste to half of Europe, the great teaching and nursing orders of the nineteenth and twentieth centuries were being born through the determination of a handful of women. The late Holy Father, St. John Paul II, called the new millennium, the "springtime of the Church" and so there are signs that a regeneration has begun.

However, to understand the fragile sprigs that have been and are budding through the forest of decay, ruin, and stasis of the twenty-first-century Church in America, it is necessary to lay out the constituent elements of the idea of personal renewal in classical Christian thought, and how, through many controversies and tortuous steps from the writings of St. Paul through four centuries to the writings of St. Augustine, the Church hammered out the radical doctrine of personal reform.

A summary of that discussion in the next two chapters will form the context for a description of the rebirth of Catholic religious communities in the United States.

V

A Millennial Journey:
The Search for Sanctity

The eminent British historian, Sir Herbert Butterfield, wryly observed that the doctrine of original sin was the only teaching of the Christian Religion that was empirically verifiable.[30]

Aside from psychopaths and other clinical outliers (like barely intelligible existentialists), I do not see how anyone can challenge that statement. Every time someone expresses a regret, blushes over a remembered gaffe, is overwhelmed by remorse for a past evil wished or done, smugly balloons with pride over something accomplished and then is later embarrassed by it, clothes himself or herself in the cape of self-righteousness in commenting on the failures, malevolences, and depravities of others—these bear witness that we are not what we wished we were.

This is leaving aside such prosaic musings as wishing to be wiser or more handsome or healthier or richer or whatever else we sense poignantly as a shortfall over which we repine. From the murkiest shadows of paleontology until today, all human beings and everywhere have perceived this fundamental intuition. In fact, the complete absence of remorse is an irrefragable proof of psychosis.

Penitentiaries for the criminally insane are filled with such people.

Concomitant with this intuition is the second intuition that there was (is?) probably a time and place where and when the gap between our current awareness of self and an image of what we wish we were existed or exists. (Without this perception, the corpus of science fiction literature would be immeasurably thinner!) In some inchoate way, we know that we are deficient in *human integrity*. Our instant awareness of this entails a belief that we were once different from what we find ourselves to be at this time.

Further, we have another intuition that, in some way or another, we can—and should—aspire to regain that state of integrity that has been lost. The sensible person's moral reason also holds out some vague intuition that our current state of moral defectiveness was somehow precipitated by our own choice. It flies in the face of human decision-making to conclude that, on the contrary, it has all been determined and inexorable and there is nothing to be done about it although this stark determinism has enjoyed bloomlets of credibility from time to time in various cultures.

Aside from the undiluted version of predestination in its earliest and classical formulation in Calvinist theology wherein it was necessary in order to safeguard the utter sovereignty of God and some of the more primitive natural religions such as that of the Aztecs, no culture has taken this position to be one of practical social policy.

In many cultures these ruminations led human beings to envisage a range of archetypes: a "special place" or a "golden age" where everyone is beautiful and the sun is always shining; there are never any tears and justice reigns everywhere. In the Christian dispensation this is known as the state of original justice, and it is expressed in the story of Eden found in the opening chapters of the book of Genesis

In addition, in most ancient cultures and in all the great religions, there is also an identifiable event—a catastrophic fall from justice—in which human integrity is shattered forever. The modes, methods, and personalities involved vary from culture to culture and religion to religion, but the ingredients are similar: a state of preternatural bliss, some type of test or challenge, a wrong choice willfully done, and the imputation of a loss of personal integrity that passes on into the human race bringing in its train all the evils to which we are heirs.[31]

Out of these mythic elements, the ancient cultures and religions—East as well as West—fashioned the fundamental principles of the moral life, that is, that feature of human activity that deals with becoming or reclaiming the integrity lost through making choices that diminish or enhance human excellence. The moral dimension of a human being thus constituted the lifelong search for the restoration of human integrity. In the earliest stages this dimension was enveloped in stifling mythologies and esoteric religious rituals and ceremonies, attended by acts of mortification or atonement to inure oneself against evil forces and to assuage or placate those forces that would provide solace or rescue from the travails of this world.

Perhaps it might be a ritual of purgation or it might be a "special place" in which a type of purification took place or where the gods resided and thus imparted "secrets" of the good life to the properly disposed. While this magical world of gods and incantations gave plausible explanations concerning questions of good and evil and provided litanies of "Dos and Don'ts", it failed to satisfy "inquiring minds" as the National Inquirer proclaims. As human reflection deepened, the understanding of moral choices became more sophisticated, morphing out of ritual and mystery into a proper illumination of the internal structure of moral options based on a developed anthropology focusing on the question, what is a human being?

To their everlasting glory, the disassociation of rational inquiry from hoary myths and arcane religious practices concerning human action emerged among the early classical Greeks. Already by the time of Hesiod in the eighth century BC, widespread skepticism had undermined the credibility of the ancient Greek gods.[32] By the fourth century BC with the emergence of Plato and then Aristotle, rational inquiry had moved to center stage in the pursuit of an understanding of the moral life. In the *Meno*, Plato describes Socrates' search for virtue or the elements of a good life and whether it can be taught. It becomes a means of overcoming one's deficiencies and thus, permitting a person to become "good."

The argument evolved into what is the modern—and fallacious—idea that ignorance is the ground for immorality or injustice and that knowledge is the avenue to virtue, and hence, the good life. While the *Dialogues* cover a range of topics, it would not be an exaggeration to say that the leitmotif of the vast majority of them is the eternal quest for rational harmony and the attainment of human integrity.

What is it? How do we attain it? What must we do to

retain it?[33]

In Aristotle the locus of virtue, or the moral life, was rooted in the capacity of a human being to reason, and thus to be able to infer from the rational ends of human action; namely, to do that which is in conformity with human nature at the right time, for the right reason, in the right way, and toward the right person. Moral choices were not singular; they were tissues of relationships and proportions all of which are *essential* in doing a "good" thing. The *Nicomachean Ethics* is a sublime meditation and a handbook at the same time analyzing in detail what all human beings aspire to (happiness) and what are the means and modes by which it can be achieved.

Unlike the characters in the *Dialogues*, Aristotle sets out to present a pragmatic and thoroughly sensible statement about the etiology of the moral life. It is, after all, the life of a human being in action and leads either to happiness or increasing levels of disorder and chaos in one's personal and social life. The fact that each year thousands of people continue to learn the rudiments of the moral life from a study of the *Nicomachean Ethics* twenty-five hundred years after it was written attests to its persistent realism and usefulness.

These were not the only expressions in classical thought about the moral life. The Stoics taught that human happiness consists in the effort to still all passions and to be equally stolid in the face of tragedy and in the face of success. The Epicureans highlighted the values of the pleasure/pain principle. They understood this idea at a more sophisticated level than mere hedonism or sensuality but rather as a kind of harmony among the competing feelings and emotions in which an attained stasis conduces to human welfare and happiness.

By the end of the classical era, virtually every school of thought concerning the moral life had been developed in some form or another. Of all the fields of human learning, it was the one in which, arguably, the ancients did their best work.But it must be remembered that classical learning was highly aristocratic—that is, it had little impact on the great masses of humanity in the ancient world. The learned in the famous Greek city-states, and later the governing classes of the Roman Empire, imbibed deeply of these philosophical "schools", but they were an exceedingly small minority.

The millions of people who constituted classical society adhered to all kinds of religious practices and rituals; some of great antiquity; others remarkably new and novel. For many, the gods still lived and worked among human beings. Read about St. Paul's encounter in Ephesus with the devotees of the goddess Artemis (for whom Ephesus was *the* center of the classical world) to see how seriously the common people of antiquity took their gods and goddesses. It is well to keep in mind Gibbon's sardonic comment in the *Decline and Fall of the Roman Empire* regarding religion in the classical world: "The gods in the ancient world were considered by the people as equally true, by the philosophers as equally false, and by the magistrates as equally useful."

As it did in virtually every other realm of human thought, Christianity had a profound impact on the human understanding of the moral life. I think it can be safely said that in no other aspect of human experience did Christianity make such a dramatic impact. It did nothing less than turn the pursuit of moral excellence and human integrity on its head.

And, as with so much else of trembling pregnancy in Christianity's emergence in the Age of Augustus, the source of a new vision of humanity and its destiny begins with a reading of St. Paul's Epistle to the Romans, the theologically rich and most complex of his letters.

St. Paul paints a bleak picture of the human condition: given to their baser instincts, men and women are awash in sin and in a state of rebellion against God.34 The law is the very sign of their rebellion and their condemnation. Nor do any type of moral calisthenics or rational typologies, arcane rituals, or secret initiations free them from their just punishment. In fact, Paul dramatically announces that there is *nothing at all in human effort that can effect even the beginning of a return to a state of natural integrity*. The corrosive effects of original sin are so devastating that we are born and remain in a state of rebellion from which, by our own efforts, we cannot escape.

Yet, after having painted this dismal picture—certainly far worse than anyone can find in classical literature or philosophy—Paul turns to announce that through the salvific work of Jesus Christ it is possible to achieve something greater than the *restoration* of human integrity. In fact, the opportunity has been made available to become nothing less than a member of God's own family.35

This is a remarkable *tour de force* that will imprint itself on all reform literature and action from then until now; undoubtedly, even to the end of the world. It is counterintuitive to the highest achievements of rational analysis and discourse attained laboriously by few over the centuries. What St. Paul announces is that a new power has been unleashed in the world; a power that at one and the same time scalds away the scales that hide the true nature of our sinfulness and the lurid and hell-destined character of our very selves, and makes available a destiny—*for every man and woman*—that far exceeds the aspiration of all the thinkers who ever reflected on the moral life.

Paul in effect calls us to a higher ambition than a *restoration* of human integrity. Left to ourselves we seek nothing better than to find a way back to what has been lost.

St. Paul says, "That's too modest!"

By virtue of the redemptive act of Christ, an entire new world and a heretofore unheard of and unthought- of aspiration of union with God has been made possible. The "good news" was nothing less than the entrée to a reality—the ultimate reality—which we could never have anticipated nor on which do we have any claim either by right or effort.

As with so much else of the Gospel, it would take centuries for the clarity and centrality of this teaching to be anchored at the heart of personal reform. To the classical mind—ignorant of the salvation story found in the Hebrew Bible—much of St. Paul's message was opaque. It was as if Paul had revealed the destined end of the human journey and only sketchily limned the processes to attain it.

Given that much of the Epistle to the Romans deals with the relationship of the Jewish-Christian community in Rome to the Church at large as well as their (and his) own Jewish traditions, gentiles new to the faith would have a hard time grasping the old dispensation and its relationship to the new dispensation. Threading the path from the lofty proclamation of the good news to personal sanctification would be a long one. Articulating the steps along the way would take a host of brilliant minds and three full centuries of modeling and disputations.

It must be remembered also how fragile and beset by problems the early Christian communities were. Planting the Gospel message in the apostolic age took heroic effort. There had been martyrs from the beginning; starting in Jerusalem with the beheading of the apostle James and the stoning of St. Stephen the Martyr in whose death St. Paul himself played a role. During the early years of the patristic age, the Church was periodically devastated by the capricious, yet sanguinary persecutions launched by the Roman government; more relentlessly as the imperial crisis of the third century deepened and the Diocletianic autarchy sought to stem internal dissolution while confronting an ever-larger number of external and formidable enemies.

The Church's growing pains were further exacerbated by the rise of the great heresies almost from the time of its origin: Montanism, Marcionism, Gnosticism, Manichaeism, Donatism, Arianism, Pelagianism, and a dozen lesser, equally aberrant sects roiled the early Christian communities; in some cases for generations. (At one point, the *majority* of the entire episcopacy were confirmed Arians, and the great champions of the faith were languishing in one or more of their repeated exiles.)

A few of these will be discussed later where their impact on the idea of reform was an important consideration in the process of establishing the features of genuine reform.

Some of these heresies involved titanic struggles about the central beliefs of the Christian Faith: the person and nature of Christ, the organization and authority of the Church, the canon of scripture, the role of the Virgin Mary in the Christian constellation, and the never comfortable relationship between the Church and the state both before *and* after the Constantinian settlement. It was hardly an environment in which the nuanced theological reflection on the relationship between Christ's salvific work and one's personal journey to human integrity or sanctification could be worked out.

This radical sundering of the classical understanding of human integrity and how to confront its loss was nothing less than a new anthropology. It liberated the human from the old cosmology of a balance between cosmos and chaos, chance and reason, determinism and apparent freedom, and portrayed a creation contingent and maimed by sin yet sustained and redeemed by an infinite and pervasive love.

This new anthropology also uncovered a network of relationships unknown in the classical world. It gave an explanation of the origins of creation taking an insight of the Jews and projecting it onto a universal stage. It shattered the concept of a recurring cycle of events endlessly repeating themselves in never-ending, meaningless recurrences.

Rather, Christianity invented "time" and invested it with a new and dramatic focus: a beginning, a middle, and an end in a sequence of never-repeatable, dramatic events upon which literally hung the eternal felicity of every human being in the history of the world from beginning to end. Not incidentally, Christianity transferred the locus of the search for human integrity from the "outside" a human being—the structures of the world, the framework of society, the ineluctability of fate, the sibylline books, the entrails of chickens or what have you—to a radical interiority. Paradoxically, the road to human integrity was both accessible to all and simultaneously utterly unattainable through any human effort.

It is impossible to discuss the idea of reform in the early Church without a cursory examination of the great theological controversies of the first four centuries because it was often in adumbrating a particular character of the "good life", or the perfection of the spiritually saved, that people found themselves outside of the traditional teachings of Christianity.

The first major heresy of the patristic age was that of Montanism. It can serve as a prototype of the many that followed. Montanism maintained that God spoke through his "chosen ones"; Montanus (naturally!) being the one most preferred by God. He further taught that his prophecies superseded the teaching of the apostles, and thus his "new way" offered a shortcut to salvation by severe moral strictures and, of course, following Montanus and whatever further prophecies would be revealed. Had not Tertullian fallen into the Montanist heresy toward the end of his life, Montanism would be less familiar today.

It is, however, instructive as revealing some of the recurrent characteristics of heretical movements, then and now... and into the future until the last trumpet sounds. First, there is a strong or charismatic leader who, often working within the tradition, illuminates an attractive path for leading a Christian life.

Second, there emerges the acolytes or disciples whose adulation often becomes overwhelmingly attractive and serves as invidious comparisons to the lay about, conventional Christians. Third, there is often an innovative teaching that purports to explicate something heretofore undiscovered. This precipitates the voices of criticism and prudent caution, which might be dismissed as envy or self-serving.

Soon, a certain truculence and sense of persecution transforms into self-righteousness and defiance. Last, follow the obligatory denunciations, demands of unquestioned loyalty, and the exile of all save the most slavishly devoted. Unless buoyed up by some powerful external support, such as the Counts of Toulouse in the case of the Albigensians or the German Princes in the case of Lutheranism, the remnant passes onto the slagheap of history.

The Gnostic heresy, for example, was basically an attempt to provide a means to access mystic knowledge through an abstruse philosophy of the life of perfection. The heady combination of excessive rationalism and a theophany of inner and mystical illumination become a growing sign of a school of thought; holding out to the faithful the "only true" access to perfection. Much like the Montanists of the second century and the *illuminati* of the sixteenth century, these teachings affirmed the erroneous belief that some—and only some—were selected for divine gifts and teachings.

The Gnostics appealed to several basic human traits as well as recurring themes in classical thought:

(a) the sense of dislocation from an original and a to-be-reclaimed state of life from which human beings were alienated;

(b) that by stint of discipline and earnest study, the path to true happiness could be discerned;

(c) that while all might strive for this illusive goal, it was attainable only for the "elect," the identification of whom was an exasperatingly difficult, if well-nigh impossible, task;

(d) the unattractive human emotion of being drawn to the charms of exclusivity and the concomitant separation of the great "unwashed."

The Gnostics also enjoyed increasing membership because it was a movement that was comfortable with the varied oriental cults that emerged in the closing decades of the pre-Christian era and which were to radiate and find adherents throughout the empire in the age of the Caesars. Gnosticism, like all theophanies, appealed to people— and there were thousands of them—who were benumbed by materialism and flabby conventionality of a decadent classical culture. It was heroic, mysterious, exclusive, and made you look smart; fatal attractions to the rootless and the bored.

Falling on the other side of the orthodox divide were the Pelagians and the semi-Pelagians who, mesmerized by the apparent efficacy of human action being able to perform good and meritorious deeds, leapt to the conclusion that eternal bliss was attainable principally, if not solely, through human exertion. Moreover, they short-circuited the Christian understanding of anthropology and sin by denying the doctrine of Original Sin. This permitted them to repudiate the idea that Christ's death had any redemptive value and was, at best, a "good example". They also affirmed, as logically deduced from their premises, that it lay solely in the realm of human choice to attain a state of perfection.

The Pelagians were particularly popular in the fourth century after the Constantinian settlement, which saw the ranks of the Christian community grow by leaps and bounds. The removal of the fear of martyrdom was a marvelous spur to the conversion of pagans, and the fourth-century Church teemed with the newly converted whose motives were often dubious at best. These countless thousands who considered Christianity hardly different from the now-repudiated gods and goddesses of antiquity and perhaps only a cut above magic were an affront to the zealous, and there was no group more affronted than the Pelagians who preached a rigorous moralism as the only mode of the Christian life. They were particularly disturbed by the crass ritualism of many of the newly converted and excoriated them for not reforming their lives since, as they taught, attaining moral perfection was within the ken of every Christian simply by their own motivation.

One of the constituent elements of many, if not all, of these early heresies (and which would reappear in later heresies as well) was an evident rigorism. And the classical example of rigorism was the Donatist heresy of the early fourth century. The Donatists, deeply rooted in the Church in Africa, maintained that those who abjured their Christianity during the great age of the persecutions of Diocletian had forfeited their fellowship in the Christian community and could in no way be restored to membership.

Their loss of grace was absolute and irretrievable. In the case of apostatizing priests and bishops, the Donatists insisted that their recantation of the faith resulted in the loss of all their sacramental powers—forever—so that they were unable to forgive sins, confect the sacrament of the Eucharist, ordain men to the priesthood and so on. So attractive was this posture to the latent righteousness of many that, at one time, a majority of the African bishops were confirmed Donatists. From these positions of power, they were able to harass and persecute the orthodox bishops, even those who had remained steadfast in their faith and had survived the Roman persecutions.

Another characteristic of these early heresies—more prominent in some than in others—was an unconscious or even conscious Manichaeism; overly stressing the duality of spirit and flesh and often rendering an unsophisticated explanation of some of the more energetic passages in St. Paul's Epistles, especially Romans and Galatians wherein the conflict and contrast between the spirit and the flesh is most forthrightly stated.

Many of the divergent movements in the Church from the earliest times, sooner or later, related the reacquisition of human integrity to a turning away from what was denounced as carnal activities. But for the "elect" these activities included not only the traditional litany found in the scriptures—gluttony, sodomy, fornication, theft, adultery, and the like—but also marriage, friendship, and often all kinds of edibles that would have made a Carthusian regimen appear opulent.

The paradox of many of these groups was that having become convinced of the righteousness of their cause, they often lapsed into some kind of antinomianism asserting that having been "grace-filled" and "chosen" they were exempt from the strictures that bound ordinary mortals and thus all things were permitted them. Hence, one finds from the earliest orgiastic sects down to the present day a heartless rigorism regarding the moral habits of the unredeemed yoked to the practice by the "elect" of the most flagrant sexual scandals imaginable.

While in the early centuries, these sects in many ways mimicked the pagan practices in the more cosmopolitan centers of the classical world where temple worship was hard to distinguish from routine prostitution and organized orgies, it remains true that a moral theology that has gone off the rails is a fatal and tempting alternative for Christian behavior as the Anabaptists of Münster in the 1530s and the Jonestown suicides in the 1970s attest.

Whatever more weighty conclusions can be derived for a review of the great heresies of the patristic age, it certainly reveals that laying out the path to personal reform and the re-creation of human integrity was a task with enormous risks and fatal detours.

Before moving on to the orthodox resolution of this critical question, some mention should be made about the rise of monasticism both in the East and in the West. In sum, it was a practical effort to live a Christian life in a civilization exhausted and besieged, over which ruled a government alternatively and increasingly repressive and ineffective. If Tacitus sourly reflected in the early decades of the Empire, "The more numerous the laws, the more corrupt the government," he would have deemed the late Empire as one of the most corrupt in history.

Ironically, in 212 AD, the Emperor Caracalla extended Roman citizenship to all the inhabitants of the Empire.

What at one time had been deemed a precious right avidly sought, now became the avenue to expand an ever more burdensome tax system and to enlarge the conscription rolls to recruit an ever more sullen army.

By the time of Diocletian (284–305), the coinage had been debased, the laws had been multiplied beyond measure, workers were tied by law to their occupations, and three generations of violence and war had sapped the vitality of the Roman state. A massive administration, staffed by legions of bureaucrats, crushed the remaining centers of any entrepreneurial spirit left in the commercial system, and the telling conversion to Christianity of hundreds of thousands over the last two centuries seemed to have created an independent and unassimilable structure in the metropolitan centers of the Empire.

The catastrophe of the third century, when order was frayed, life was cheap, and hardly an emperor died of natural causes, held little charm for those who aspired to a more focused and telic spirituality. Prayer and solitude were difficult to sustain in a weary world filled with distractions, noise, systemic violence, and cascades of dreary news.

It was known from the earliest times that prayer and solitude were the fundamental tools of a vibrant spiritual life. The Gospels record many occasions when Jesus withdrew to a secluded spot to pray and spend time with the Father. This was a clear typology that could be easily emulated, if not easily practiced.

The early eremites who fled to the Egyptian desert sought out a life alone with God by fasting and solitude, a daily regimen to subdue all earthly desires, and prayer. Thus were the essential ingredients of the ascetical life born.

A cursory reading of Athanasius's life of Anthony—one of the first prominent solitaries in the third century—gives a vivid description of his career of living twenty years alone in southern Egypt. Others in time, heartened by his holiness, came and built huts in the vicinity and a rough outline of a community began to take shape.

Later in the century, Pachomius (the Great), in northern Egypt, organized a community of solitaries and gave them a primitive rule. This is usually identified as the beginnings of the formal monasticism that was to become such a profound influence in the shaping of early medieval life in Europe.

The public life of the Empire was so unappealing and the desire for sanctity so overwhelming that first hundreds and then thousands sought refuge in the wastelands of Egypt and the deserts of Syria and Palestine. So rapid was the growth of eastern monasticism that, by the latter half of the fourth century, the Emperor Valens felt compelled to evict the thousands of monks from Egypt.

While in part this was probably due to his own commitment to Arianism, there is little doubt he was also determined to bulk up the working and hence tax paying members of the Empire. When he was defeated and killed at the Battle of Adrianople in 378, the displaced monks, of course, construed this as a sign from God.

Monasticism in the west is generally identified as beginning with St. Martin of Tours who upon being selected as Bishop of Tours established a simple hut outside of town and lived there during his episcopate. He gathered around him three or four laymen who also lived the eremitic life. So successful was the monasticism he established that it was said over a thousand monks attended his funeral in November 397. Monasticism spread throughout Gaul in the fourth and fifth centuries and reached the British Isles where an early form of Celtic monasticism flourished.

The significant development of monasticism in the West is rightly identified with St. Benedict of Nursia, the son of a noble Roman family who, in abandoning Rome to seek a more Christocentric life of prayer and solitude, withdrew south of the city to Mount Subiaco, the site of ancient Roman ruins dating to the time of Nero, and founded the monastery of Monte Cassino. He gathered around him some followers and wrote a rule, half of which is devoted to developing a strong Christocentric spiritual life and half dedicated to dealing with the organization of the community.

The Rule of St. Benedict became the foundation stone of the growth of Western monasticism in the succeeding centuries. Its genius, richness, focused common sense, and simple rules for community organization were to spawn successive reforms in the history of the Church: the Cluniacs, the Cistercians, the Camaldolese, and the Trappists, among the most prominent, aspired to live more authentically the mission of the Rule in changing environments and times.

Let us now resume the search for a developed theology of the Christian life that charts a path from the words of Scripture to a mature statement of the relationships among human beings as they were first created. What really happened at the Fall, where do we go from there, and how do we get there?

Given the radical event of the Person of Jesus Christ and

his singular role in time and space, it should be no surprise that the thinkers of the early Church struggled with language in trying to describe those "Christ-events" and their impact on human beings. It was clearly seen by the Greek and Latin fathers that foremost the salvific work of Christ atoned for the sin of Adam and all the sins of mankind that followed upon the original sin.

But was there anything else? Could not the efficacy of the Crucifixion and the Resurrection permit a world free of the consequences of sin? Now Christians had before them clear understanding of what a world without sin would be like. One had only to turn to the opening chapters of Genesis where the state of preternatural man possessing human integrity is described.

Hence, the first inference about human destiny, advanced by Origin and developed by Gregory of Nyssa, was that of *restoration*; that the work of Christ was to ensure that after death those who had faithfully lived the Gospel would inhabit an Edenic world; that the great disruptive stain of sin would be eradicated and a state of original justice would be *restored*.

The sense of restoration (or *apocatastasis* as Origin called it) found a sympathetic echo in the waning world of pagan philosophy and cosmology because it seemed to mimic the notion of a return to a golden age from which, mysteriously, human beings have fallen. The intuition of personal and universal disaggregation and eventual restoration is a powerful one because it not only resonates with each person's honest grasp of his or her moral life and moral failures and struggles but also satisfies a strong though inchoate feeling that there was once a place where all lived in harmony and peace.

But scripture passages—always pregnant with multiple meanings—could lead to variant perceptions of the future. Jesus consistently preached, "Repent, for the kingdom of God is at hand!" What was the "Kingdom of God"?

It did not appear to be a geographic entity. So, was it an invisible community of the righteous? If so, it still remained illusive in the understanding of the regeneration of the moral life of human beings. It was not difficult in musing on these features of the Christian message to be tempted into a view of a kind of heaven-on-earth or golden end-times.

It was in the patristic age that the seeds of millenarianism first flowered. If the Kingdom of God was at hand, it must mean *at hand*—at the end of history; since we live in the end-times then it follows that that stage is next. Thus, the Kingdom may represent a terrestrial world in which Christ rules over all the just.

Whether it was an event with a determined time period or was destined to exist forever was the source of energetic but not very illuminating controversies in the third and fourth centuries. (Those familiar with the legions of devotees of the *Left Behind* mania will find this all too familiar.) We must bear in mind that in the early Church the belief in the imminent end of the world was quite common.

Read the letter to the Thessalonians to learn as to how people were preoccupied with this issue. Like recurring deviancies about the nature of the moral life, prognosticating the end of the world was—and is—an ever-tempting preoccupation of Christians of a particular sort, from the Thessalonians to the establishment of Seventh Day

Adventism, which, after so many embarrassing failures, seems finally to have abandoned efforts to pinpoint the date of Armageddon.

Yet even now, I have no doubt that some drudge in a run-down apartment in Los Angeles is attempting, once again, to parse out of the Book of Daniel, the day of doom.

But I digress.

While the controversies often hinged on a specific meaning of a Greek word in the scriptures and might entail decades of writing (much time and effort . . . and words were expended in illuminating the difference between "likeness" and "image" found in the two accounts of the Creation in Genesis, for example), they nonetheless attest to the long gestation period required before the Christian community could articulate a coherent world view of the relation of Eden to this world and both to the hereafter. After all, eschatology is probably to theology what brain surgery is to medicine.

Was the drama of history to result in the restoration of a perfect past; an earthly kingdom of the saints; a fusion into the image and likeness of God from whom the existence of each human being begins?

Another view, again drawn from a reading of scripture, was that to regain human integrity it was necessary to be purged of materiality and to once again become a pure spirit like God who is the ground of each of our individual creations. It was in the context of this controversy that the wrangling over the meaning of likeness and image, cited above, took place. For those Church fathers immersed in the Platonic and Neoplatonic traditions like Origin, the concept of reuniting each individual spirit with God bore a striking resemblance to the concept of the forms in Platonic thought wherein resides the pure perfection—and reality—of all the facsimiles in the world, which are really pale imitations of the true.

One of the clearest expressions of this view was found in the aphoristic reflection of Gregory of Nyssa: "The definition of human beatitude is the assimilation to God"[36].

A more contemporary pair of eyes would see this as akin to—but not necessarily the same as—the great oriental religions and theophanies that aspire to reduce multiplicity to oneness by dissolving into the One and losing all individuality.

The Greek Fathers also spent a good deal of time attempting to explicate the idea of the Kingdom as found in the scriptures. The Kingdom was "at hand", but it was "not of this world" as Jesus told Pilate. But, then, what was the relationship of the Kingdom and the world? Their thinking developed this in an analogical manner that connected some of the new themes of Christian life and renewal with some of the ideas of royal governance that, in the East, had great antiquity.

In Eastern Christianity, the monk rather than the secular priest became the exemplar of the highest form of the Christian life, and to the extent that he participated in the life of Christ he shared in Christ's kingship. With the evolution of the Constantinian settlement in the fourth century and the adoption of Christianity as the religion of the Empire under Theodosius in 381, it was not difficult to see in the new Christian emperors the image and likeness of God himself; the Christian Empire, in a sense, becoming the prototype of the Christian life.

Eusebius of Caesarea advanced this argument most explicitly in the fourth century in the reign of Constantine. Just as Christ is the King of Heaven and the *Logos* of the Father, so the Emperor is the King of Earth and the Word of Christ. And as all men and women are called each into a special relationship with Christ, so are they also called into a special role in the Christian Empire.

The sacramentalization of the late Roman Empire and the blurring of the lines between immanence and transcendence became defining characteristics of Byzantine Christianity and the culture it created for a thousand-year period. Eusebius further maintained that the constant renewal and reform of the Christian life was the principal responsibility of the Emperor, and that citizenship in the Christian Empire was the tangible consequence of choosing to pursue a Christian life.

This monastic and imperial model received a severe challenge in the writings of one of the greatest of the Greek Fathers: St. John Chrysostom (347–407), first as Bishop of Antioch and then as Patriarch of Constantinople. He was probably the first thinker to develop the idea—later taken up by St. Augustine—that the priest not the monk was the true exemplar of Christ in the community or the kingdom of the family; that, in fact, we are all, in a way, "kingly" to the extent that Christ dwells within us and he does this through the ministration of his priests.

Moreover, spiritual growth and personal reform were personal responsibilities of each and every one of us. In this, he was anticipating, in a way, the Second Vatican Council's teaching that we are all—without exception—called to a life of holiness. Thus, over and against the imperial and monastic model, Chrysostom proposed a model of reform and renewal that was civic or communitarian and priestly, the very elements which St. Augustine would use in crafting his own synthesis in the late fourth and early fifth century.

In spite of his heroic efforts to preach a new kind of reform and to reform the clergy in his Patriarchate, St. John enjoyed little success. In attacking some of the more questionable practices of the imperial court he aroused the hostility of the empress, who was not long in creating a political alliance with some of the worldlier of the Byzantine bishops who resented St. John's denunciations of *their* lifestyles.

Not surprisingly, he was hounded out of his patriarchal see and died in Pontus on his way to exile in present-day Georgia. He was as popular and well loved by the common people of Constantinople as he was resented and opposed by the imperial and ecclesiastical party. It was with an uncommon amount of evidence that he could declaim, "The floor of Hell is paved with the skulls of bishops!" And this less than a century after Christians were being torn apart by wild beasts in the Roman Colosseum! Power and privilege, especially for clerics, as we've seen above, are fast working toxins.

G. Ladner himself provides the best summary of the Greek Fathers in the following words:

"In its interpretation of Scriptural terminology and ideology of renovation and reforms, Greek patristic thought emphasized above all the restoration of the creational integrity of the universe and of man and the terrestrial representation of original God-nearness in a world order upheld by the ruler and the monk."[37]

While the Latin Fathers mined many of the same ideas from the scriptures *in re* personal reform as the Greek Fathers, they, however, marked out several new lines of thinking on this question. It was in the Latin Fathers of the fourth century, particularly Arnobius and Lactantius, that the idea of *in melius reformare* was first broached, in an inchoate form.

We first find here the idea that personal reform may not consist simply in a return to a former life of perfection, though Lactantius, for one, did at one point in his writings affirm this to be the case. He maintained, nonetheless, "a life of virtue lived among evil and suffering is of greater value than even a return to primeval bliss and innocence."[38]

The reorientation from a glorious "past" to an indeterminate "future" was a special insight of St. Ambrose. He used the calling of Abraham by God to a new life a typology of the universal call to sanctity for every human being. The "call" itself was not itself a state of perfection, but the beginning of the journey, which for Ambrose, ended in a union with Christ.

His second momentous contribution was the idea that man's return to paradise—to the state in which Adam existed before the Fall—while laudatory, was in itself, inferior to the arrival in the kingdom of Heaven; a position more in keeping with the Pauline insights of Romans and Galatians. Ambrose proceeded to elaborate the idea that what Christ did was not simply to reopen the opportunity to re-enter the state of paradise in which Adam resided, that is, simply to restore the "grace of nature", but because he was God and his act of supererogation on the cross and his subsequent Resurrection infused the order of nature with an infinite grace this permitted nothing less than humanity's participation in the very family of God as his adopted sons and daughters.

It was this insight that led Ambrose to characterize the Fall as the *felix culpa*.

Thus, grievous as Adam's sin was in terrible consequences for the entire human race, had it not occurred, there would have been no need for Christ to have come and, thus, we would not have received the opportunity to enter into the intimacy of the Trinity, which—now—is the pledged reward for our fidelity.

Last, in recognizing St. Ambrose's contribution to the development of reform, we need to review his famous controversy with Symmachus, who, at the behest of the pagan senatorial party, called for the restoration of the Altar of Victory in the Curia of the Roman Senate on the grounds that its antiquity would help to ensure the future of the Empire. In obliterating Symmachus' arguments, Ambrose rebutted the notion that antiquity, of itself, conferred some prescriptive right, that in fact, the world had progressed from the time of its creation to evermore enhanced levels of development and growth.

Moreover, there was nothing metahistorical about the Roman Empire and that God had not conferred on her some transhistorical meaning that exempted it from the insights of Christianity or the ravages of history. Christ himself proclaimed that *he* was the beginning and end of all things—the alpha and the omega—and that it was in fact the Church and not the Empire that was the *depositum* for the development of the Christian life. Through the priesthood and the Sacraments, Ambrose contended, each person could find the means to enhance his/her life of grace, to participate in the celestial life of God and that everyone— from the emperor to the lowliest peasant—was a citizen of this spiritual world.

In this Ambrose also departed from the Eusebian concept of equating the Kingdom of God with the Christian Empire and struck the first systematic blow for the *libertas ecclesium* that was essential to live out a life of personal reform. And that was to be a recurring theme of civil theology all the way down to the writings of John Courtney Murray and the Second Vatican Council.

By now, all of the major ingredients for constructing a mature and comprehensive theology about the nature of personal reform and its locus in the economy of salvation had surfaced; what remained was to put them together in the proper manner. The principal architect of that endeavor was to be the thinker who most influenced the subsequent millennium of Christian thought, St. Augustine.

VI

On Augustine and Personal Reform

In the year 430, the Ostrogoths under the leadership of Alaric I sacked the imperial city of Rome. It was the first time a foreign invader had occupied the ancient capital of the Empire since the Gauls seized it in 387 BC over 800 years before.

While the damage was relatively light (Alaric was not interested in destruction; he was interested in participation), the psychological impact was profound. From one end of the Empire to the other, it was conceived as an iconic event, unprecedented in the half-millennial sway of Roman rule over the civilized world of the Mediterranean basin.

The ranks of the Roman pagan aristocracy, already assaulted by a century and a half of civil war, social disorder created by religious persecution and the eventual triumph of an alien religion, reeled before the awareness of the fragility of all the principles of classical culture to which they clung. The foundations of the world seemed to have collapsed beneath them.

What was to be made of such a devastating event? What did it portend?

For many of the ruling classes, it was unmistakable

evidence that in abandoning their ancient gods and embracing a religion (Christianity) that focused so fervently on the next world and evinced a sustained irenic outlook about this world, they had forfeited the mantle of historical ascendancy and jeopardized that eternality of the *city* that Virgil had so eloquently described in the *Aeneid*.

What was to be expected of a regime that first moved the seat of government to the eastern half of the empire, clothed it in quasi-oriental panoply, and then closed the temples on the Palatine and doused the sacred fires of the temple of Victory in the Forum? The sack of Rome to them was the logical consequence of civic apostasy.

In a lengthy response to the Roman (and Christian) tribune in Rome by the name of Marcellinus who had bruited these ideas in his own letter, St. Augustine laid out the seminal concepts that were to form the architecture of his most expansive work, *De Civitate Dei (The City of God)*. The first twelve books of the *The City of God* are devoted to a careful refutation of the assertions made by Marcellinus in his letter; the remaining ten books are an unfolding of nothing less than the Christian understanding of human history from its origins in the creation of the universe and of Adam and Eve until Christ's Second Coming at the end of time. It aspired to impart a comprehensive understanding of all human history as the unfolding of God's providential plan of salvation.

Since there are many erudite commentaries on *The City of God*, I will limit my treatment to those features that are relevant to this study.[39]

Taking the fall of the bad angels as a point of departure,

Augustine describes the origins and development of two cities: the City of God and the City of Man, the former composed originally of the good angels as well as subsequently by those who live in grace and who, historically, have been participants in the unfolding of providence in time through a love of God; the latter made up at the beginning by the bad angels and then those who, after the fall of Adam and Eve, pursue a life of self-love.

In fact, for Augustine the very finality of love is crucial to the understanding of the difference between the two cities and thus to advancing an explanation of human history. "Two loves have then made two cities, love of self unto contempt for God the earthly city, but love of God unto contempt of self for the heavenly city."[40]

St. Augustine asserts the proposition that fundamentally there are really only *two* loves and that the numerous variants of love we experience can be related in some form or another to one or the other of these two loves. In Christian theology, love is defined as the willful choice of the good for another—to use the classical terms. Thus, when we say "I love you," what we should mean is that I *will* the best good possible *for you* regardless of the consequences *to me*.

It is this sense that one speaks of "emptying oneself for the sake of another" as St. Paul says Christ did for the sake of all men and women.[41] It is what any human being does in demonstrating the generosity of surrender of self for the good of another; say, in the classic example of a soldier who sacrifices himself on the proverbial hand grenade to save the life of his comrades or, in a less dramatic fashion, when a spouse foregoes a promising career to spend years raising a family.

But this kind of love finds its ultimate ground of being in the love of God himself, the *amor Dei*. It is to love God Himself for His own sake since He is love itself—as St. John says—that we are able to love anything… for its own sake and perfection.

On the other hand Augustine says is the *amor sui*, the love that has as its ultimate object not God but *oneself*. Such love can *appear* disinterested, altruistic, sentimental, affirming, laudatory, noble. However, it can also *be* acquisitive, exploitative, cruel, disingenuous, and sinister.

The point is that these are *variants along a continuum* and not opposites since the ultimate purpose is to will the good for oneself and not the glory of God. The key, then, is not *that* we love, but *why* we love. We deliberately blind ourselves to this by designing utterly conventional categories of what are acceptable activities deserving honor and which are unacceptable activities deserving avoidance (often based on some calculus of self-interest) which rest on no philosophical or theological grounds whatsoever.

Much of modern literature is an enormous allegory in illuminating this aspect of modern life; the drunken priest in Graham Greene's *The Power and the Glory* comes immediately to mind. Are the sacrifices one makes for another done so for the love of God or ultimately for self?

Even when we are altruistic or noble or laudatory, we need to be clear as to why we are so; we need to dig under the surface, so to speak, and get into the recesses of the human heart, as the psalmist says, to affirm what ultimately is the object of our love: God or ourselves. St. Paul's celebrated paean to genuine love in the Epistle to the Corinthians clearly demarcates the snares of a distorted sense of love: "If I hand over my body so that I may boast, but do not have love, I gain nothing."[42]

Given this understanding of Augustine's idea of love, let us return to its role in *De Civitate Dei* for it is nothing less than this: the motivating engine of each of the two cities. The City of God is the community in time of all those who have as their ultimate focus, the love of God.

Augustine tells us that it is along this thread that the providential course of history runs. The raising up of judges, then kings, then prophets in the Hebrew Bible, followed by Christ and the saints in the New Testament, and thereafter are all the unfolding of the Divine Plan of bringing all creation, and most especially men and women, to a state of perfection. It is the City of God that is a true community of those who love God and through which grace gushes into creation, perfecting a wounded nature and cleansing it of sin.

This rendition constituted a radically new sense of time and of history, neither of which played a significant role in classical culture. As was mentioned earlier, Christianity introduced a previously unimagined understanding of history as being pivotally important.

This rendition constituted a radically new sense of time and of history, neither of which played a significant role in classical culture. As was mentioned earlier, Christianity introduced a previously unimagined understanding of history as being pivotally important.

Whereas for the classical mind, history or time was simply the trivial succession of discrete events repeated in large and recurring cycles, for Augustine, and indeed for Christianity, it was the dramatic locus—telic and unrepeatable—wherein God wove all things toward his own glory. It was not the stage on which heroic men struggled against the necessity of nature or of fate as so eloquently described by the Athenian tragedians, but an arena of free choices and eternal consequences in which each man and woman moves toward or away from the love of God and ultimate beatitude or soul-crushing alienation forever.

It is further illuminating to note that Augustine chose the word *city* deliberately. It bespoke several strands that he wove together. First, the primary intuition is that all human beings are by nature relational beings. They enter the world in a community—the family—and they mature and live in the larger community of family, friends, acquaintances, and associates and, indeed, the rest of the human race.

Second, for centuries, the classical world had extolled the life of the city as the most appropriate in which humans dwell. So decisive was this in the Greek mind that the Greeks distinguished themselves from those beyond the pale by two specific features: those people did not speak Greek and they did not live in a *polis* or community. Hence, they were "barbarians."

Third, the sense of *communitas* most clearly mirrors the corporate membership of all human beings in the Mystical Body of Christ in which the living and the dead are united by ties of grace extending from the beginning of time and continuing into eternity.

Fourth, the alternatives such as the "kingdom" of God or the "reign" of God entailed other meanings that created ambiguity or led to confusion such as the tendency of some of the eastern fathers to equate the kingdom of God with the emerging Byzantine Empire, that is, the Christian Roman Empire established by Theodosius.

It is also important to understand that the *City of God* is not coterminous with the Church. The Church is simply Christ extended in time, holy and indefectible, serving as the channel of the life of grace, which is necessary for personal reform. While it is without sin, there are sinners in it.

Using the parable of the wheat and chaff from St. Matthew 13, Augustine insists that the Church is not the *City of God* because its membership is composed of those who are members of the city of God as well as members of the city of man.

Moreover, in opposition to some of the Greek fathers, especially Eusebius of Caesarea, he also insisted that there was no essential identity between the Christian Empire (after Theodosius) and the City of God. The emperor no less than the lowliest peasant is called to submit to the life of grace and to pursue his personal reform through the ministerial offices of the church, namely, the sacraments, prayer, and discipline. This was dramatically displayed when St. Ambrose of Milan excommunicated Theodosius (he who established Christianity as the religion of the empire no less), after perpetrating the massacre of the citizens of Thessalonica.

In addition to ensuring the uniqueness of the City of God, Augustine closed the door to Christian millenarianism as a legitimate metahistorical proposition. No physical entity in this world can or ever will equate to the City of God.

To Marcellinus and others in the Roman patrician classes, Augustine responded by stripping away the transhistorical or meta-historical significance that they imputed to the Roman Empire. Yes, it was unfortunate that the city of Rome had been sacked, but it was due to the simple vicissitudes of earthly power and not to some quasi-religious apostasy.

The hubris of world dominion can bring about unanticipated disasters. Augustine spoke feelingly of Rome's magnificence and contributions and the earnest desire that it would continue to be a force for good in the world, but that it, no less than any other power, was subservient to the pervasive direction of God's providence in history and when it had fulfilled the purposes for which it had existed it would fade away as all of its predecessors had.

The City of God needs to be understood as the pilgrimage of those who love God; they are wayfarers in an alien land for their goal is not of this world, echoing the words of Christ to Pilate at his trial. The ministerial priesthood serving as *alter Christi* in forgiving sins, providing the Eucharist, preaching the Gospel, and giving counsel, sustains them, for it is Christ alone who does these things through them.

Augustine, in a sense, envisages the course of a human life to be the intersection of two lines on a plane: one, rising from left to right and the other descending from left to right. These conform to the natural downward course of aging and bodily decay and the upward growth of spiritual richness as a member of the City of God.

Paradoxically, however, the Christian life revealed by Christ permits a human being to realize a much greater goal than a return to the pristine state Adam enjoyed. The Resurrection of Christ reveals that we are all destined inheritors of a glorified body in eternity, something that was not vouchsafed Adam.

Augustine explicates this idea in this contrast: "For the impossibility to die is one thing... the possibility not to die another."[43]

After all, Adam possessed *the possibility not to die,* but the consequence of his sin was that he did die... as have and will all human beings, the legacy of his original sin. However, the transformational work of Christ makes available *the impossibility to die*; that is, we are destined to eternal life with a body unlike Adam's. Our glorified bodies will reunite with our souls after our deaths. This was a significant development of one aspect of personal reform.

The second important development by St. Augustine was the idea that the trajectory of our personal spiritual growth is *virtually infinite.* The channels of grace flowing from Christ not only allow us, in some way, to retrieve the virtues infused in the first man and woman but also allow us to grow in a Christic identity that is ever richer day by day.

Augustine anchors this concept in St. John's vision of the New Jerusalem adumbrated in chapter twenty-one of the Book of Revelation. What John foresees is a splendiferous world inconceivable to human thought; an abode that far exceeds the wildest imaginings of even the saints. The end of human destiny thus eclipses even the most idealized image of the Garden of Eden.

This for Augustine was the most startling news of the Gospels. Not merely that the original transgressions of Adam and Eve had been made up by the sufferings of the cross and, truly, the death of God on Calvary, but the subsequent Resurrection of the same Christ granted to every man and women literally a *new order of creation* heretofore unimagined.

This is what Paul sought to teach the Ephesians when he told them, "… that you should put away the old self of your former way of life, corrupted through deceitful desires and be renewed in the spirit of your minds, and put on the new self, created in God's way in righteousness and holiness of truth."[44]

Augustine sees this not in an allegorical fashion but a genuine new order of reality made possible by the true Resurrection of Jesus.

Moreover, as St. Paul told the Corinthians, "the dead will rise incorruptible and we shall be *changed.*"[45]

Thus it is that the Christian revelation is pretty clear that what God has in store for those who love him bears even less than a glimmer of how man and woman lived in the state of original justice. Human integrity will be reclaimed—and restored— but in an entirely different manner than was ever conceived.

As mentioned above, the growth in holiness or sanctity is an infinite trajectory. In that sense, the status of the saved is truly dependent on the level of love evinced in the pilgrimage in this world.

This intuition was given poetic form in dramatic fashion in the third part of Dante's *Divine Comedy*, the *Paradiso*, where the hierarchy of persons on the various levels of heaven reflects the level of sanctity and conformity to the will of God each demonstrates.

It does not come as a surprise then to find St. Francis of Assisi higher up the journey than St. Thomas Aquinas because in St. Francis sanctity trumped learning; and the Blessed Mother who resides in the Empyrean itself along with St. Bernard because these two exemplify the love for God, exceeding even that of

St. Francis. Thus, did Dante try to give form and texture to the basic Christian belief that the more we love God, the closer we will be to him.[46]

With these reflections Augustine laid to rest forever the three-century-long debate about whether human happiness resided in some return to the state of original justice or in something else. The members of the City of God are destined for a fullness of life far beyond what was provided to Adam and Eve.

As he mentions in the *City of God*, "… this mortal life shall give place to one that is eternal and our body shall be no more this animal body, which by its corruption weighs down the soul, but a spiritual body feeling no want and in all its members subjected to the will."[47]

In this he echoes St. John's statement in his first letter, "We are now the sons of God, and it has not yet appeared what we shall be. We know that when he shall appear we shall be like him, because we shall see him as he is."[48]

In the age of the Fathers, this search—and debate—about human integrity was framed in the language of restoration (*renovatio in pristinum*) and renovation (*renovatio in melius*). That is, was the salvific work of Christ achieved in order that we might be restored to the state of original justice as found in Eden before original sin or to a better life than that? In the magisterial work of Augustine, the answer to that question had been decisively given. We are now destined for a world we cannot even imagine; to be forever in the presence of God.

He further terminated the perennial search for "special" knowledge or for mystical rituals as means of accessing the road to human integrity. Personal renewal was a community journey of those who love God and who are sustained through the channels of grace—scripture, Sacraments, and magisterium—provided by the church that slowly but assuredly performs that gradual transformation of each of us into a "Christ-lover."

After all, Jesus was most clear when he told his disciples, "This is my commandment: Love one another as *I love you.*"[49]

In sum, St. Augustine contextualized the teaching found in St. Paul's Epistles and absorbed two centuries of theological reflection in creating a comprehensive explanation of the singular events of the Hebrew Bible and the life of Christ; events which the mind of the classical world considered idiosyncratic and completely irrelevant to the world of classicism.

Just as the Exodus was (and will always remain) the archetype of the relation of God to creation and of being called and not merely a quaint melodrama about an ancient and marginalized people, so the Crucifixion and Resurrection of Jesus were lifted from being a regrettable but common execution of a popular teacher on the periphery of the empire and anchored as the *central events* of all time.

All that came before—sacred and secular—was a prelude and a preparation, as all the church fathers, eastern and western, taught, and all that comes after those events is the working out of the providence of God and the building up of the City of God.

Thus personal reform is the vocation of every man and woman, for it is the only means by which the regeneration and sanctification of the world can go forward. This was resoundingly reaffirmed in the Second Vatican Council when the Church declared that for everyone there is a universal call to holiness. [50]

This call is the only means by which we as pilgrims, jostling with the citizens of the City of Man, can shed the sustaining vices and tendencies that constantly distract us, and often successfully, from our intended goal. It is the only means that *permits* God to work in our souls to fashion a "new creation" worthy of participation in the Beatific Vision, that new reality made possible and made known by the Resurrection.

As all of the great reforms in the church through the centuries attest, the sustaining power of a new charism provided by God is essentially tied to the intimacy of each man and woman of a community to the person of Christ, living all the while with the conviction that *this* relationship establishes the meaning of our other relationships in this world and not vice-versa.

Even a cursory familiarity with the life of Thérèse of Lisieux lays bare the profound intimacy she had with Christ. The richness yet crystalline simplicity of that relationship, earned in great part through suffering and detailed in letters and books and most evidently in her claustrophobic life in the Carmel at Lisieux, persuasively convinces one that she deserves the title Doctor of the Church formally proclaimed on her centenary by John Paul II.[51]

Likewise, if one reviews the life of St. Teresa of Ávila one is struck by the closeness and casualness of her continuous conversations with Jesus; often more intimate and frank than all of her other conversations. Her *Interior Castle* can also well serve as the prototype of the journey we are all embarked on, moving from one room to the next, often in the face of trials, drawing ever closer to our appropriate end.[52]

* * *

We have moved through a lot of territory from the shadows of the Neolithic age when the first stirrings of religious sentiment can be documented through the enormously significant events strewn through the history of the Jews and the wondrous creation of classical culture and the birth of Christianity. We have toured the rousing controversies as the church began to formulate a sophisticated understanding of its beliefs in the face of the challenges of a senescent classicism and thousands made the first halting efforts to establish a relationship with God through the monastic and cenobitic traditions. A long "flyover" of the reform movements in the modem world down to our present time highlighted models of success and eventual decline.

Now in the new millennium, which John Paul II called the "springtime" of the new evangelization, we are witnessing the emergence of the perennial striving for personal reform in the dozens of religious communities that have been established in the last thirty to forty years.

Like the anchorites of third-century Egypt, the communities of monks in Byzantium as well as in the West during the emergence of the barbarian states as successors to the Western Empire, the early Capuchins and Ursulines, then the Notre Dames and the Sisters of Mercy and their countless colleagues in the nineteenth century, there are new "hidden" and "unknown" groups of men and women here in the United States who, like their ancient counterparts, are either deafened by the noise of culture in decay or pained by the suffering of fellow human beings who are neglected and lost.

And, quickened by a host of new charisms, are once again manifesting the imperceptible grace of providence and the work of the Holy Spirit in the human journey to a new life around the Throne of God.

We will now see what forms these are taking.

VII

The Complexion of the New Sanctification

Before examining some of the new religious communities that have emerged in the last four decades, it will be helpful to delineate some of the pervasive qualities or features that are virtually universally present among them all. From the most contemplative to those that are the most socially active, certain characteristics seem to be shared to some degree or another.

Identifying these will help illuminate the general nature of the *new reform* and give us an insight into the motivations and sustaining power of these new communities.

First, they are profoundly Christological and, in a sense, highly vertical. Regardless of their charism, these communities began—and continue—with a deep, personal, and active relationship with Christ. It is the unconditional affirmation of Christ as the source, summit, and *raison d'être* of their lives that is the first step taken. It is a radical disengagement from their varied circumstances, families, or environments—literally everything—that draws them to seek out men and women who share this radical commitment.

In the most existential way possible, these are people who take literally Christ's injunction that "whoever does not give up mother and father, indeed their very selves, for my sake, is not worthy of the kingdom" and "he who does not lose his life for my sake is not worthy of me."

Yet, a word of caution, for this is not a univocal commitment but an analogical one. We often quickly conclude that those men and women in the past who most effectively did this were people like the monks of the desert or perhaps St. Francis of Assisi embracing "lady poverty" and forsaking all else. Then we unconsciously arrange all of the other holy men and women in some sort of descending hierarchy to the extent that they are closer or farther away from that paradigm.

But a radical Christology cannot be confined to one model. The radical interiority of a Christ-centered life need not ineluctably lead to only a Franciscan model. It can, in fact, take a whole variety of forms and so it is analogical, leading to different kinds of actions in different circumstances.

Damien of Molokai, Angela de Merici, Ignatius of Loyola, and hundreds of others started with the same radical Christology, but they did not become Franciscans. Their emptying themselves for the sake of Christ was as equally authentic as that of St. Francis, but their lives of action led them into dramatically different apostolic endeavors. If we recall a comment from earlier in this book about St. Teresa of Calcutta, we may more clearly understand this more complex mode of analogical Christological commitment.

St. Teresa always insisted to her sisters that their lives were not primarily to care for the poor and forgotten but to daily renew their radical commitment to Christ; hence, the two hours a day in adoration and then to find Christ in the poor and forgotten.

In another case, we routinely—and rightly—laud Angela de

Merici because of her groundbreaking work in the education of young women, but as she repeatedly stressed in her colloquies to her companions, it was daily adoration of Christ that was the bond and purpose of the Ursulines; then they could go out and teach girls in the community.

Traditional religious communities in various states of decline share a language that has passed from what I would call the 'fully personal'—and absolute priority—to the notional. It is the contrast between "Yes, yes, but" and "YES!" It is impossible to exaggerate how important this is in the history of reform in the church or how absolutely essential it is to grasp the radically unconditional character of Christ's call to the life of perfection. All the great movements of reform from the time of St. Anthony to now have this in common: an unconditional and personal relationship with Christ.

By verticality, I mean an equally deep and personal commitment to God in all his transcendence. A novice focuses on his or her "creature-ness" as simply the fruit of an infinite Divine love in token of which each person's pilgrimage is a journey of returning and surrender. Not by abstruse metaphysics but by an outpouring of grace do they *know* the radical dependence each of them has on the Creator for their very existence and continuity.

If for these men and women, Christ is the ground of their being, then union with the Divine Presence is the culmination of the Christian life. They see the world and all of their circumstances through the prism of eternity. They also integrate a palpable sense of liturgical time, meaning that heaven is not a some-day-in-the-future event, but one into which they have already begun a journey.

C. S. Lewis once said that what we see depends on where we stand, and if one stands within the mantle of eternity, one sees things much differently from those who stand principally in this world and all of its attendant activities.

Thus their prayer life, be it individual or communal, long or short, is in a sense, a "wedging open" of eternity into the world, and so their apostolic labors, regardless of what they may be, are an extension of that eternal *time* into contingent time. Harkening back to the Augustinian praxis, their grace-driven lives are incremental means to widen the scope and membership of the city of God in history.

Again, as in the case of the Christocentric nature of their religious vocation, we cannot over emphasize how important this is in their lives and works. People in such communities literally see the world, time, history, themselves, in a very different way from the rest of us. They strive to bring their focus to *see as God sees*.

A second characteristic of these new religious is a different sense of community and solidarity from what one finds in older religious communities, a different sense in regard to the Universal Church as well as toward their co-members. There is, in almost all cases, an explicit commitment to the Holy Father and the local ordinary. They celebrate the occasion of the approval of their organizational documents by their bishop and, equally important, by the Holy See. They affirm a strong identification with the pilgrim church worldwide and offer themselves as instruments of its universal call to evangelize the world and sanctify creation.

It is interesting to note that a number of these new communities had very peripatetic odysseys in their earliest years often in hindsight to have been providential. One community began in Africa and ended up in Florence, Italy. Another launched in Oregon and ended up in Pennsylvania. A third started in Connecticut and ended up in Kansas City. Yet another community started in Vietnam and ended up in Lincoln, NE.

And so it goes, always disposed to respond to the call of grace and be in a place where they can serve the Universal Church; often, as in times immemorial, answering the call of a bishop to meet a need they did not even know existed.

This strong sense of solidarity reinforces their dedication to something larger than themselves, to a community of service. Two striking examples demonstrate this.

Ignatius of Loyola concluded that the Society of Jesus should have as its mission to work in the Holy Land and bring Christianity to the people of the lands of its origins; to systematically bend every effort to convert the Mohammedan world to Christianity. When it became obvious that the obstacles to this endeavor were almost insurmountable and he sought counsel from the Holy See, he received tepid encouragement and was asked to consider an alternative area of activity: education.

Ecclesiastical authorities had noticed the impressive structure of the curriculum Ignatius (and others) had devised for the formation and education of the members of the Society, tried, and modified through the 1530s and 1540s.

Could such an educational framework be adapted to the larger lay community? Might what had worked so successfully in the *Collegio Romano* be reconfigured for a larger, general population?

Ignatius and his successors took up this heretofore not considered endeavor. Through the 1570s and 1580s, revisions and adaptations were made. Finally, by 1599, the Superior General of the Society, Claudio Aquaviva, SJ—after years of testing and revising, promulgated the *Ratio Studiorum*, which became the fundamental document of Jesuit collegiate education until the early years of the twentieth century.

By 1739, there were 669 Jesuit Colleges operating in Europe, and their impact on the society and culture of Europe was incalculable. As a footnote, Ignatius's original aspiration was finally achieved when the Jesuits opened Baghdad College in 1932 at the request of Pope Pius XI. This eventually evolved into Al-Hikma University and flourished until it was seized by the Iraqi government in 1968.

Frances Xavier Cabrini was born in Italy in 1850, the last of thirteen children. Even in her early life, she was drawn to a religious life with an aspiration to work in the mission fields of China. Refused acceptance by the Daughters of the Sacred Heart of Jesus, she became the headmistress of an orphanage and gathered around her a small community of like-minded women. In 1880, they made vows and formed the Missionary Sisters of the Sacred Heart of Jesus. She attracted other women and established additional orphanages and schools in Italy. As need emerged, she experimented with health clinics and outpatient clinics and then hospitals.

The success of these endeavors brought the Missionary Sisters to the attention of Leo XIII. In 1877, in an audience with the Holy Father, Sister Francis Xavier pleaded with His Holiness to assign the sisters to the mission fields in China. He demurred and suggested an alternative.

This period was the high tide of European immigration to the United States. Among the many Europeans new in America, there were sizable communities of Italians whose burgeoning numbers far outstripped the available resources on site to address the vast needs of the Italian communities. I

t was not something to which Mother Cabrini had given much thought. After consultations with her sisters and with her bishop, Mother Cabrini, in 1889, led a contingent of nuns to New York to a new type of mission field. Her tasks were immense, and her challenges were enormous, no less from the principally Irish bishops as from the general Protestant population of the country.

Nonetheless, with considerable effort she and an increasing number of companions established schools, orphanages, clinics, and hospitals in New York, Chicago, Philadelphia, Seattle, Des Moines, and several other places throughout the nation. No sooner were these enterprises underway than she led successful efforts to replicate her successes throughout South America, especially Argentina and Brazil, which had experienced their own waves of Italian immigrants in the closing days of the nineteenth century.

These two examples exemplify the resiliency and docility of celebrated founders who found themselves, surprisingly, launched on enterprises far removed from their own initial expectations. Yet who with little hesitations responded with alacrity to the promptings of grace in discerning the needs of the Universal Church.

New communities have also revived the classical sense of community as in living in common. They are aware how critical a community life is essential to sustain the charism of their community because it is through the communitarian nature of their praying that they maintain their vitality and their reason for existing.

It is remarkable to find religious orders, even in active apostolates such as teaching or health services, who gather through the day for prayer, including in some cases, even the Divine Office, not to mention Mass, the Rosary, Adoration of the Blessed Sacrament, and scriptural reading and meditation. Equally important are their shared meals and recreation. Unlike declining religious orders, these men and women do not need to center their community life on the care and maintenance of their older members since many of them, if not most, are still in the active years of their apostolate.

Yet some of the foundations that started at the beginning of the period under review by now have acquired members near retirement; however, the vitality of the order is such that a steady influx of new members sustains an equilibrium that permits them to keep a vibrant community life of prayer and action; one in which their recently retired members actively participate.

A third feature of these new communities has to deal with the entire issue of symbolism, something at once so superficial and so profound. I think it can best be illuminated by a contrast; first, a little history and then a story. In the aftermath of the Second Vatican Council, among the many changes undertaken by women and men religious was a slow or fast alteration of dress.

For some, the stereotypical habit of the first half of the twentieth century disappeared overnight; for others, there was a quiet evolution through phases. The underlying reason given for this change was to remove the radical formalism of highly stylized garb, to throw off artificial distinctions and to appear more compatible with the general communities in which they were and would continue to work. No doubt for a number of women who entered the religious life in the 1930s and 1940s, the traditional habit was an outward sign of identity without much of an interior correlative.

No one will ever know how much of the abandonment of the religious life in the 1960s and 1970s resulted from this exposure of a superficial identity. Nevertheless, for the vast majority of women it was perceived as a step in the right direction: one less thing to have to explain, one more step in appearing normal in the world, one less barrier between persons and the message. It was the most striking, initial manner in which to convey the idea that the church was not a set of rituals but a community eager to engage the world.

In the economy of the history of reform, it will never be possible to determine what, if any, the causal impact of the change in habit had on encouraging or discouraging prospective candidates to the religious life or was a determinant for those who stayed or those who left. As recounted earlier, the motives for change and turmoil in religious life after the Vatican Council were due to a number of interacting factors, most of which no one could have anticipated.

Now, to the story.

Several years ago, I was on a pilgrimage and one of the stops along the way was a retreat house, a substantial part of which was completed—indeed, even occupied—but an addition was being anticipated on the rear side of the building as witnessed by the construction that was still going on.

The tour director asked us to stop before entering so that she could call the director of the retreat house and ask her to give us a tour. The tour director took out her phone and made a call.

Suddenly, in the distance, a major-construction-sized backhoe came to a halt. The driver reached for her cell phone and stood up. There was something incongruous about the scene that wasn't immediately evident until one of the more perceptive among us said, "I guess I've never seen a nun on a backhoe with a cell phone in her ear and, at the same time, wearing a full Franciscan habit."

It was the reversal of the meaning of symbolism. From "I am wearing this habit because I am a Franciscan" (or whatever) to "I am a Christ-centered person living simultaneously in this world and in the next, and I show that by my distinctive garb."

One can see the same thing in a panoramic scene of religious women in the church in Africa. On almost every occasion, regardless of the setting—remote, backwater shanty schools or contemporary health clinics in major urban centers—the religious women are invariably dressed in the distinctive clothing of their particular order.

A fourth characteristic which these communities evince, and which was alluded to above, is the capacity to take immediate action when facing an unexpected set of circumstances or an opportunity impelled by grace; to go, literally, where they know not but the prompting is clear and consistent.

I submit this characteristic flows from the interior capacity to see things *sub specie aeternitatis* so that even in the fragmented and ever-changing earthly circumstances they find themselves, they maintain their essential contingent character and do not close in upon the will and intellect when making a decision.

A couple of examples may demonstrate this.

In 2005, Bishop David Ricken of the Diocese of Cheyenne, Wyoming, announced his intention to establish a unique college in his diocese, Wyoming Catholic College. Situated in Lander, Wyoming, it welcomed its first class in 2007. Two features made the college distinctive (aside from being the only Catholic college in the state).

First, it welcomes new students each fall with an Outdoor Leadership Program, an extensive two-week wilderness experience to foster a strong sense of community, to begin the road of mastering the cardinal and theological virtues, to teach the habits of leadership, and to inculcate a deep appreciation of nature and all creation.

Second, it provides a classical curriculum based exclusively on the Great Books. The curriculum is common to all and there are no majors. Each student upon completion of the course of study receives a bachelor of liberal arts.

The college has been blessed with a growing and enthusiastic student body, drawing students from many states of the country. Its quarterly Distinguished Lecture Series attracts well-recognized Catholic scholars across the broad range of subjects found in the curriculum. It manifests every quality that a new founding needs for successful years ahead. It draws students from across the nation and has annually exceeded its projected goals of enrollment. Its enthusiastic parents and supporters demonstrate their commitment in sufficient financial backing so that World Council of Churches (WCC) can remain faithful to its charter decision to never accept any public or government funding in support of its efforts.

A second example of what might be called providential serendipity is the establishment of Our Lady of Clear Creek Abbey in the Diocese of Tulsa, Oklahoma. The origins of the Abbey go back to a special program established in the 1970s at the University of Kansas. The program was an in-depth study of Western civilization called the Pearson Integrated Humanities Program (PIHP). It was funded through a grant from the National Endowment for the Humanities.

The rich texture of the study was quite successful in drawing a large enrollment of students; a number of whom, discerning their path in life, felt called to the monastic life. They journeyed to the Abbey of Notre Dame de Fontgombault in France to undertake their course of study. A Benedictine abbey affiliated with the Solesmes Abbey, where the great revival of Gregorian chant began in the early twentieth century, the monks of Fontgombault give their whole lives to the chanting of the liturgy and to silence and manual labor. Their faithful adherence to the Benedictine ideals that were first practiced in the sixth century in central Italy probably had much to do with their celebrated growth in the late decades of the twentieth century.

By the 1980s, the Abbey of Fontgombault, contrary to the dramatic decline of religious vocations in Europe and America, was burgeoning with novices. In fact, the numbers were getting too large for the Abbey to accommodate and active efforts were made into finding new prospects for another site. Those members who had participated in the PIHP program at the University of Kansas had long asked that consideration be given to an establishment being made in the United States.

After canvassing several sites, their desires were fulfilled when in 1998, the Abbot of Fontgombault entered into negotiations with the Diocese of Tulsa, Oklahoma, to purchase the Clear Creek ranch with the intention of establishing a monastery on it.

From the beginning, the monks were committed to erecting a major facility that would endure—as Solesmes, Fontgombault, and even Monte Casino—into the indefinite future and would provide the same spirit of contemplation, hidden life, and liturgical celebration that those famous abbeys had done and continue to do. At first, the original founding monks converted horse stalls in cells and changed the original barn on the property into a chapel. Through unanticipated and generous donations, the monks were able to move to the phase of commissioning plans for a stone and brick facility to be the site of their community.

In the first phases, a resident wing and gatehouse were created, then the foundations of the abbatial church were laid and the walls began to rise. In 2010, the Abbey was declared a freestanding community, de jure, and was officially called Our Lady of Clear Creek Abbey. In its brief history, like its forbearer, Clear Creek continues to grow. By now fifty monks are in residence.

The Abbey of Clear Creek continues to advance its plan to be a center of prayer for centuries. Through continuous streams of unsolicited financial support the great buildings of the abbatial campus reach to the sky. Through the circuitous pilgrimage of those long ago college students at the University of Kansas to a rural horse farm in western Oklahoma, providence has had no little part to play in this story.

In the high plains of the American West, far removed from the deep Catholic centers of population, these two examples are witness to several things: the profound faith of their founders, the commitment to entrust their lives and futures to the continuing support of grace, a firm determination to perdure into the future, ever faithful, regardless of the character and quality of the larger culture in which they find themselves; much as those early missionaries nurtured the values of Christ and the remnants of ancient civilization in the collapse of the Dark Ages.

One is reminded of Macaulay's paean to the Catholic Church: Centuries hence, when a lone pilgrim from New Zealand pauses on the banks of the Thames to paint the ruins of St. Paul's, the Catholic Church will still be growing and vibrant.

* * *

In bringing this chapter to an end, it seems fitting to highlight a final—and preeminent—quality of the new religious orders: the sense of joy. St. Thomas begins his examination of the moral life in part II of the *Summa* by affirming that the end of the moral life is joy; the full and appropriate actualization of everything a human being is meant to be. As the spiritual writers down through the ages have noted, that state of perfection is only attainable in an intense communion with God.

As St. Irenaeus remarked, the "Glory of God is a man fully alive!"

There are intimations of that in our new religious communities. Members of the Missionaries of Charity, working in some of the most godforsaken places on earth, are almost invariably smiling. Members of the Priestly Fraternity of St. Peter exude an exuberance as much in their recreation as in the chanting of the Latin Mass. Women who are members of the Dominican Sisters of Mary, Mother of the Church—a community barely a decade old—has a hundred Sisters with an average age of twenty-eight. Where we see them in the classroom, at Eucharistic Adoration, or their hour of meditation, they convey an aura of harmony, spiritual richness, and joy.

This sense of joy bespeaks a live, working relationship with Christ. Through their prayer life and their active ministry, whatever it may be, they reveal, what we have spoken of earlier in this chapter, a perspective of living *sub specie aeternitatis*. They have, not just in a metaphorical sense, one foot in heaven already. Through their commitment to Christ, they have already begun their journey to sainthood for they are permitting themselves to be formed into that "person fully alive" which only God can create. Their sense of dress is a proclamation that their life is not their own, but that, like St. Paul, they announce *it is not they who live, but Christ who lives in them.*

In the words of an old spiritual master, human beings live on two planes, the vertical and the horizontal, and the joyful life is sought in establishing the proper relationship between the two. The proper relationship is first, the vertical, that is, the appropriate connection between a human being and his or her Creator.

If this fundamental metaphysical and spiritual connection

is not correct, it makes no difference what the relation of the horizontal to it is. It will not be in a proper order and the growth in sanctification will be impeded.

The second relationship is to attune the horizontal to the vertical. Our lives on this earth are lived for God. In Bishop Barron's words, "we are hardwired for God." The world, on the other hand, counsels us to make our way and peace with the world and then fit God into that; precisely backward from the Christian life.

These new communities get this clearly. As broad as is the range of their ministries, they all begin by fixing the vertical relationship with God and then turning to whatever activity God points them toward to begin the journey to sainthood. It is in that cluster of decisions that they wedge open a door to heaven.

FOOTNOTES

1 - The psalms are replete with acknowledgements of God's active role in the world. In addition the writing of numerous saints attest to the active role God plays in the lives of those to whom He reveals himself. This reality wherein God "resides" so to speak, lies beyond the reach of human reason to grasp. It is appropriately the realm of Faith. For an explanation of the relationships between these two modes of knowing, a good place to start would be the encyclical by John Paul II, Faith and Reason, 1998.

2 - For example, in 1850 there were 1,600,000 Catholics in the United States being served by 1,320 priests, many of them itinerant "castoffs" from French dioceses, often with very rudimentary language skills. The ratio increased barely perceptibly by 1870 when there were 4,500,000 Catholics being served by 3,780 priests, most of whom were foreign-born. Daniel-Rops, Henri. *The Church in the Age of Revolution*, New York: E.P. Dutton & Co., 1965, 362-368.

3 - Arroyo, Ramon. *Mother Angelica: the remarkable story of a nun, her nerve, and a network of miracles*, New York: Doubleday, 2005.

4 - One of the finest literary assaults on this world-view can be found in the novels and short stories of Flannery O'Connor, especially *Wise Blood*, *The Violent Bear it Away*, and *A Good Man is Hard to Find*, wherein frightening and violent actions are used to shatter social and personal conventions and permit the play of grace in achieving a kind of redemption.

5 - This is a kind of summary sentence from "35,000 feet" of the architecture of St. Thomas' Summa Theologiae, which describes God and creation and its eventual return to Him.

6 - Richard Rorty (1931-2007) taught at Princeton, Virginia, and Stanford and published several philosophical works in the analytic and pragmatic traditions that expressed a deep skepticism about truth propositions. Peter Singer (1946 –) is Professor of Bioethics at Princeton and is best known for his book, *Rethinking Life and Death*, New York: St. Martin's Griffin, 1996, in which he anchors the "good" of abortion in denying that it is the taking the taking of an innocent life. He also has advanced the idea that animals have "rights" that can, in certain cases, have priority over human life. His views are not without controversy.

7 - Fr. J. Bryan Hehir is on the faculty of the Harvard Divinity School and Georgetown University. He is currently the Parker Gilbert Montgomery Professor of the Practice of Religion and Public Life at Harvard. He is also Secretary for Health Care and Social Services of the Archdiocese of Boston.

8 - Hillerbrand, Hans. *The Protestant Reformation*. NewYork: Harper & Row, 1968.

9 - Beales, Derek. *Prosperity & Plunder: European Catholic Monasteries in the Age of Revolution*, Cambridge University Press, 2003.

10 - An old but still excellent account of this 'evolution' of the revolution into more radical phases was well described by Brinton, Crane, *Anatomy of a Revolution*, New York: Prentice Hall, 1952.

11 - *Wittberg, Patricia. The Rise and Fall of Catholic Religious Orders: A social movement perspective. SUNY Press, 1994.*

12 - Though its tint and tone betray an outdated enthusiasm for the compatibility of American Democracy with a unique form of American Catholicism, a solid historical account of the history of the Church in America is Jay P. Dolan's *The American Catholic Experience: A History from Colonial times to the Present*. Garden City, New York: Doubleday, 1987. Also important is James O'Toole, *The Faithful: A History of Catholics in America*. Cambridge: Belnap Press, 2008. Much of this summary comes from these books.

13 - Dolan, Jay P. *The American Catholic Experience*, 121-123. O'Toole called the 1st chapter of his book, 'The Priestless Church' supra, 11 & ff for obvious reasons.

14 - O'Toole, *The Faithful*, 12-13 recounts a vivid example of this in the Hanlys family. It also hints at the unique independence of the Catholics in America who lived without reliable structures and clergy.

15 - Those favoring the "roman" party were particularly heartened when Leo XIII issued his encyclical, Immortali Dei in 1881 on the two "perfect" societies, the Church & the State.

16 - This is taken from the 'history' link on the web site of the Diocese of Erie, PA.

17 - Stewart, Jr., George. *Marvels of Charity: History of American Sisters and Nuns*, Huntington: Our Sunday Visitor Publishing, 449

18 - Broderick, Francis. *Right Reverend New Dealer: John A. Ryan*, 210 ff. New York: Macmillan, 1963.

19 - Stewart, Jr., George. *Marvels of Charity: History of American Sisters and Nuns*, Huntington: Our Sunday Visitor Publishing, 449.

20 - Wittberg, Patricia, *The Rise and Fall of Catholic Religious Orders*, Albany: State University of New York, 118 ff.

21 - Slawson, Douglas J., *Ambition and Arrogance: Cardinal William O'Connell of Boston and the American Catholic Church*, San Diego: Cobalt Productions, 2007.

22 - Not that this was all so secret. When he sailed for a pilgrimage to the Holy Land and a visit to Rome on his return home, Fr. Thomas McCarthy (from Boston) wrote to Cardinal Bonzano, then the apostolic Delegate: "The majority of the priests, nuns, and seminarians are praying that he not return. His return to Boston will mean only one thing and that is that Rome approves of his mal-administration, scandalous life and hypocrisy." AASMSU as quoted in Slawson, Ambition and Arrogance, 143.

23 - Morris, Charles, *American Catholics: the Saints and Sinners who Built America's Most Powerful Church*. Times Books: New York, 1997, 123.

24 - On one occasion, when asking for a second assistant, Msgr. Bonner was told by the Cardinal, "I beg to say frankly that I do not see the need for still another assistant. Time was when one man did the entire work… and that was not so very long ago."

25 - Trusteeism was a transient movement in 19th century America in which ethnic parishes were established by the parishioners, long before formal, ecclesiastical structures were created,

and ownership of the property was invested in a group of congregants as "trustees" of the congregation.

26 - I am indebted for this biographical information on these prelates to the excellent work of O'Toole, James, *The Faithful: A History of Catholics in America*, and Carlin, David, *The Decline and Fall of the Catholic Church in America.*

27 - Wittberg, Patricia. *The Rise and Fall of Catholic Religious Orders*, 211.

28 - "With a derivative and largely unexamined self-definition that was essentially the same as that of dozens of other religious congregations, new recruits learned what religious life was by memorizing a uniform 'catechism' of received, unchanging knowledge … With equal rigor, young sisters were introduced to the order's most minute customs 'including such details as the proper way to eat a banana or crush the shell after having consumed an egg'." Wittberg, Ibid.

29 - See Nygren, David J. & Ukeritis, Miriam D., *The Future of Religious Orders in the United States: Transformation and Commitment*, 225 ff. for an excellent analysis of the eroding of foundational principles in religious life in the post-Vatican II period.

30 - Butterfield, H., *Christianity and History*, London: G. Bell & Sons, 1949.

31 - Eliade, Mircea, *History of Religious Ideas*, Chicago: University of Chicago Press, 1978.

32 - Jaeger, Werner, *Paideia: Ideal of Greek Culture*. London: Blackwell, 1969.

33 - While there are many modem translations of the works of Plato and Aristotle, one can still rely on the old classics, Jowett, B., *The Dialogues of Plato*, many eds. and McKean, R., *Basic Works of Aristotle*, many eds.

34 - St. Paul, Epistle to the Romans, 1, 16-18 ff. and 2, 1-11.

35 - St. Paul, Epistle to the Romans, 8, 14 ff.

36 - Ladner, G., *The Idea of Reform*, New York: Harper & Row, 1967, 90.

37 - Ibid., 133.

38 - Ibid., 141.

39 - There is a vast literature on Augustine but for materials in this chapter, consult Peter Brown, *Augustine of Hippo*; Marthinus Versfeld, *A Guide to the City of God*; Christopher Dawson et. al., *St. Augustine: His Age, Life, and Thought*, a collection of rich, synthetic essays by prominent 20th century writers; John Mourant, *Introduction to the Philosophy of St. Augustine: selected readings*; and Cantor & Klein, *Medieval Thought; Augustine and Aquinas*. Essential, of course, is *The City of God* by St. Augustine, esp. Books XII and following.

40 - St. Augustine, *De Civitate Dei*, chapter XIV.

41 - St. Paul, Letter to the Philippians, 2: 7.

42 - St. Paul, Letter to the Corinthians, 1: 1-13.

43 - St. Augustine, *De Genesi ad Litteram*, VI, 24 as cited in Ladner, G. The Idea of Reform. New York: Harper & Row, 1967, 158.

44 - St. Paul, Epistle to the Ephesians, 4:22.

45 - St. Paul, First Epistle to the Corinthians, 15: 52.

46 - Dante Alighieri, *The Divine Comedy* (translated by Allen Mandelbaum), New York: Alfred A. Knopf, Everyman's Library, 1995. Cantos XI, XII and XXXIII.

47 - St. Augustine, *De Civitate Dei*, Book XIX, chapter 17.

48 - St. John, First Epistle, 3: 23.

49 - St. John, Gospel, 15: 12 ff.

50 - Abbott, Walter. *The Documents of Vatican II*, New York: Guild Press, 1966. John Paul II focuses on this theme as the central message of *Novo Millenio Ineunte*, Boston: Pauline Books and Media, 2001.

51 - *Story of a Soul: Autobiography of St. Therese of Lisieux*, trans by Michael Day, Westminster: New Press, 1957.

52 - *Teresa of Avila, The Interior Castle*, New York: Paulist Press, 1979.

Bibliography

Papal Documents

Pope Leo XIII, Immortali Dei, 1881.
Pope John Paul II, Fides et Ratio, 1998.
Pope John Paul II, Novo Millenio Ineunte, 2001.

Sources

Abbott, Walter. *The Documents of Vatican II*, New York: Guild Press, 1966.

Angus, Samuel, *The Religious Quests of the Graeco-Roman World. A Study in the Historical Background of Early Christianity*, [original, New York: Charles Scribner's Sons, 1929], Biblo & Tannen, 1967.

Arroyo, Ramon. *Mother Angelica: the remarkable story of a nun, her nerve, and a network of miracles*, New York: Doubleday, 2005.

Beales, Derek. *Prosperity & Plunder: European Catholic Monasteries in the Age of Revolution*, Cambridge University Press, 2003.

Brinton, Crane, *Anatomy of a Revolution*, New York: Prentice Hall, 1952.

Broderick, Francis. *Right Reverend New Dealer: John A. Ryan*, New York: Macmillan, 1963.

Brown, Peter, *Augustine of Hippo*, California: University of California Press, 2013.
Butterfield, Sir Herbert, *Christianity and History*, London: G. Bell & Sons, 1949.

Cantor, Norman F., & Klein, Peter L., *Medieval Thought; Augustine and Aquinas*, Massachusetts: Blaisdell Publisher, 1969.

Carlin, David, *The Decline and Fall of the Catholic Church in America*, New Hampshire: Sophia Institute Press, 2003.

Coburn, Carol K. & Smith, Martha, *Spirited Lives. How Nuns Shaped Catholic Culture and American Life 1836 – 1920*, Chapel Hill: University of North Carolina Press, 1999.

Daniel-Rops, Henri. *The Church in the Age of Revolution: 1789 - 1870*, New York: E.P. Dutton & Co., 1965.

Dante Alighieri, *The Divine Comedy*, trans. by Allen Mandelbaum, New York: Alfred A. Knopf, Everyman's Library, 1995.

Dawson, Christopher, ed., *St. Augustine: His Age, Life, and Thought*, New York: Meridian Books (M51), 1957.

Dolan, Jay P., *The American Catholic Experience: A History from Colonial Times to the Present*, Garden City, New York: Doubleday, 1987.

Ebaugh, Helen Rose Fuchs, *Women in the Vanishing Cloister. Organizational Decline in Catholic Religious Orders in the United States*, New Brunswick: Rutgers University Press, 1993.

Eliade, Mircea, *History of Religious Ideas*, Chicago: University of Chicago Press, 1978.

Felknor, Laurie, ed., *The Crisis in Religion Vocations*, New York: Paulist Press, 1989.

Fialka, John J., *Sisters. Catholic Nuns and the Making of America*, New York: St. Martin's Press, 2003.

Hillerbrand, Hans. *The Protestant Reformation*, NewYork: Harper & Row, 1968.

Jacob, W. M., *Lay People and Religion in the Early 18th Century*, New York: Cam-bridge University Press, 1996.

Jaeger, Werner, *Paideia: Ideal of Greek Culture*. London: Blackwell, 1969.

Jowett, Benjamin, *The Dialogues of Plato*, Classics Club edition, 1942.

Kubiak, Hieronim, *The Polish National Church in the United States of America, 1897 – 1980: its Social Conditioning and Social*

Functions, Krakow: Jagiellonian University Scientific Journals, 1982.

Ladner, Gerhart B., *The Idea of Reform. Its Impact on Christian Thought and Action in the Age of the Fathers*, [original, Massachusetts: Harvard University Press, 1959], New York: Harper & Row, 1967.

McGreevy, John T., *Catholicism and American Freedom. A History*, New York: W. W. Norton & Co., 2003.

McKean, Richard, *Basic Works of Aristotle*, New York: Random House, 1941.

McManners, John, *The French Revolution and the Church*, New York: Harper & Row, 1970.

McManners, John, *Church and Society in 18th Century France*, 2 Volumes, Oxford: Claredon University Press, 1998.

Morris, Charles, *American Catholics: the Saints and Sinners who Built America's Most Powerful Church*, New York: Times Books, 1997.

Mourant, John, *Introduction to the Philosophy of St. Augustine: Selected Readings and Commentaries*, Pennsylvania State University Press, 1964.

Murray, John Courtney, S.J., *Religious Liberty. An End and a Beginning*, New York: Macmillan Co., 1966.

Murray, John Courtney, S.J., *We Hold These Truths*, Maryland: Sheed & Ward, 1960/20053.

Nygren, David J., C.M., & Ukeritis, Miriam D., C.S.J., *The Future of Religious Orders in the United States: Transformation and Commitment*, Connecticut: Praeger, 1993.

O'Brien, David J., *Public Catholicism*, New York: Macmillan, 1989.

O'Toole, James M., *The Faithful: A History of Catholics in America*, Cambridge: Harvard University Press, 2008.

Richardson, Cyril, ed., *Early Christian Fathers*, New York: Macmillan Publishers, 1970.

Singer, Peter, *Rethinking Life and Death*, New York: St. Martin's Griffin, 1996.

Slawson, Douglas J., *Ambition and Arrogance: Cardinal William O'Connell of Boston and the American Catholic Church*, San Diego: Cobalt Productions, 2007.

St. Augustine, *De Civitate Dei* (Concerning the City of God against the Pagans), trans. by Henry Bettenson, London: Penguin Classics, 1972/20034.

St. Augustine, *De Genesi ad Litteram* (On the Literal Interpretation of Genesis), trans. by Roland J. Teske, S.J., Washington, D.C., The Catholic University Press of America, 1991.

Stewart, Jr., George, *Marvels of Charity: History of American Sisters and Nuns*, Huntington: Our Sunday Visitor Publishing, 1994.

Teresa of Ávila, *The Interior Castle*, New York: Paulist Press, 1979.

Therese of Lisieux, *Story of a Soul: Autobiography of St. Therese of Lisieux*, trans. by Michael Day, Westminster: New Press, 1957.

Varacalli, Joseph A., *The Catholic Experience in America*, Connecticut: Greenwood Press, 2006.

Versfeld, Marthinus, *A Guide to the City of God*, Maryland: Sheed and Ward, 1958.

Ward, W. R., *Christianity Under the Ancien Régime. 1648 – 1789*, Cambridge Uni-versity Press, 1999.

Willis, John R., S.J., *The Teachings of the Church Fathers*, [original, New York: Herder and Herder, 1966], San Francisco: Ignatius Press, 2002.

Wittberg, Patricia. *The Rise and Fall of Catholic Religious Orders: A Social Movement Perspective*, SUNY Press, 1994.

www.ingramcontent.com/pod-product-compliance
Lightning Source LLC
Chambersburg PA
CBHW061145040426
42445CB00013B/1558